PRESENTED BY
THE OTHERWISE CLUB
1985

GORBACHEV

GORBACHEV

A BIOGRAPHY

Thos. G. Butson

STEIN AND DAY/*Publishers*/New York

THIRD PRINTING 1985

First published in 1985
Copyright © 1985 by Thomas G. Butson
All rights reserved, Stein and Day, Incorporated
Designed by Louis A. Ditizio
Printed in the United States of America
STEIN AND DAY/*Publishers*
Scarborough House
Briarcliff Manor, N.Y. 10510

Library of Congress Catalog Card No. 85-40232

Contents

1

A
New Kind
of
Soviet Leader

TWO INCIDENTS can serve to illustrate the way in which Mikhail Gorbachev personifies a generational shift in the men who wield power in the Soviet Union. In the first incident, Stalin would never have acted as Gorbachev did. Molotov wouldn't have either. Khrushchev might have, but never with the same degree of sophistication. But for Gorbachev in May 1983, it seemed quite natural to be sitting in front of a Canadian parliamentary committee debating nuclear arms controls, East-West propaganda programs, and even whether or not there were any Russian spies in Canada.

On occasion, as Gorbachev was questioned sharply—even rudely—by the Canadian politicians, he grew somewhat testy. But he was always under control, and behind the heat was a sometimes almost folksy humor. At one stage of the proceedings, during a discussion of the suspected Soviet spies in Canada and elsewhere, Gorbachev snapped that such reports were simply part of a scheme to discredit the Soviet Union and were not having much effect anyway.

"I will tell you bluntly," he told the Canadians, "as they say in our country, in Central Asia, the wind blows, the dogs bark, and the caravan moves on."[1]

The second incident occurred almost eighteen months later. In December 1984, Gorbachev was making a highly publicized visit to Britain. As he had during the Canadian visit, he had shown a surprising amount of self-assurance in trading arguments with British politicians and winning unusually laudatory coverage from the British press.

The talks in London behind him, Gorbachev had departed for the provinces to see at firsthand how British industry functioned. His party had reached Edinburgh, and the authorities in the ancient Scottish capital had planned an elaborate reception. But before the festivities could really get under way, Gorbachev had a bombshell for the British, press and politicians alike. At a news conference he announced the death in Moscow of the veteran Soviet Defense Minister, Dmitri Ustinov. It was not so much the news itself that surprised the British—Marshal Ustinov had been reported in poor health for some time—but rather it was the fact that a Kremlin official, normally the most close-mouthed of individuals, was announcing almost casually important news that had not yet been formally published in the Soviet Union.

Gorbachev's visits to Canada and Britain were not his first appearances in the West.

Indeed, more than any other high Soviet official outside the diplomatic apparatus, Gorbachev has made a practice of visiting foreign countries outside the usual Moscow orbit. Sometimes his trips have been the usual ceremonial visits required by the protocol of the Soviet bloc. But at other times they have been more substantial, carefully intended to widen his knowledge of Western methods and practices in agriculture and industry. And so it was in Canada; after his appearance in Ottawa and discussions there with various officials, including then Prime Minister Pierre Elliott Trudeau, he left for extended tours of cash-crop farms in Southern Ontario and ranches in Alberta.

And, during the subsequent British visit, the meetings with Prime Minister Margaret Thatcher and other officials were regularly punctuated with inspections of automobile manufacturing plants and chemical and agricultural establishments in England and Scotland.

Both visits exuded a certain air of a public relations campaign, and if that were the Russians' intention, there was little doubt that the campaign was successful. This was particularly true of the time spent in Britain, where both Gorbachev himself and his stylish wife, Raisa, were treated to the sort of media exposure normally reserved for royalty. But there was also substance in the performance. Gorbachev's visit to London had been timed to coincide with delicate negotiations on nuclear arms and weapons in space, and as the Kremlin's messenger, Gorbachev spoke forcefully on that subject. After listing some steps that had been taken to improve the climate for negotiations with the United States, Gorbachev said, "Of key importance in all this is prevention of a space arms race. Such a race would not only be dangerous in itself, it would give a boost to the arms race in other areas."[2]

The foreign trips, therefore, have been anything but junkets. For Gorbachev comes to prominence in the Kremlin in a much different fashion from most other high Soviet officials. Stalin had to spend years outwitting Trotsky, Zinoviev, and a host of other potential successors to Lenin before his claim to absolute power was beyond dispute. It took the intervention of the military in the person of Marshal Zhukov to consolidate Khrushchev in power. Leonid Brezhnev, Yuri Andropov, and Konstantin Chernenko reached their high office only after years of backroom service in the party bureaucracy, but none of them served the kind of apprentice-ship that has been given to Mikhail Gorbachev.

Gorbachev, too, is a creature of the party he joined in 1952—when Stalin was still alive—and is subject to its rivalries, but he is a new kind of Soviet functionary. Although he was born in the middle of the industrialization and collectivization agonies that wracked the Soviet Union in the 1930s, and as a boy must have known the horrors brought on by the German invasion of Russia, he was also young enough to escape the worst aspects of those ordeals. Indeed, it can be argued that those very calamities, having decimated a whole generation of Soviet citizens, made it possible for Gorbachev and others of his age group to rise to power at such a relatively youthful age. This age factor is important in another way, too. Many of the Brezhnev generation may not have actively participated in the denunciations that were an integral part of the purges of the Stalin era, but they certainly knew people who had been affected by them; and to some extent they profited by the disappearances and denunciations as they moved up the bureaucratic ladder. For this reason, they tended to be sensi-tive on the subject, ever anxious, especially in the case of Brezhnev, to build up a heroic image and past history that may not have been extremely well bolstered by facts. Where Brezhnev and his colleagues were prone to look back on past glories, real or imagined, Gorbachev and his age group are much more forward looking, taking pride in their country's very real achievements but also understanding its shortcom-ings, and confident that they can provide the remedies. The reason for this is understandable. During Gorbachev's young manhood, the Soviet Union was emerging from being a relatively backward industrial nation into becoming a world technological leader capable of sending cosmonauts into orbit around the Earth and unmanned rockets to the other planets. Moreover, Gorbachev is easily the best-educated and most sophisticated Soviet leader since Lenin. In addition to a law degree from Moscow State University, the most prestigious educational institution in the country, he holds another degree in agronomy from a college in his hometown of Stavropol. From his early days in the Komsomol, the Young Communist League, he has been accustomed to holding positions of authority, and throughout his career he has been unusually close to some of the most influential personalities of the Soviet Union, notably Yuri Andropov, Mikhail Suslov, and Fyodor Kulakov, who was for many years one of the country's and the party's most influential agricultural officials. Gorbachev is widely traveled, having visited West Germany, France, Belgium, Vietnam, Bulgaria, Hungary, Czechoslovakia, Mongolia, Portugal, and Italy in addition to Britain and Canada. For these reasons it is easy to understand the self-confidence exhibited so openly that May morning in Ottawa and in similar appearances in London.

Gorbachev might seem to have been a man in a hurry. In a nation and a government long dominated by graybeards, he has stood out as a mover and a shaker, the new boy eager to make his mark. During the tenure of Andropov as the Soviet leader, there were repeated reports that Gorbachev was being groomed as Andropov's handpicked successor. Like Andropov he had been born in the Caucasus in the area around Stavropol. Like Andropov, he first became prominent through the Komsomol. But more importantly, he was publicly associated with Andropov in the latter's celebrated campaign to combat corruption and inefficiency in Soviet agriculture and industry. Moreover, like Andropov, he gained a reputation for placing emphasis on promotion because of ability, rather than on the cronyism that was so prevalent in the later years of the Brezhnev regime. But, when Andropov died after only a relatively brief term in power, Gorbachev was passed over in the selection of a new leader, reportedly because of that very same cronyism. By most reports, the generation of Andrei Gromyko, Marshal Ustinov, and Konstantin Chernenko was still not ready to yield power to the new men in the Kremlin.

But since then, Gorbachev has grown in stature, taking charge of Communist Party ideology—a role previously held by Suslov and Andropov—and broadening his responsibilities beyond agriculture to cover the whole economy, until even in the Soviet Union it came to be accepted that he would be the next leader of the party and the government.

What sort of man is he?

What are the priorities he is likely to emphasize?

What is his attitude toward the West in general and the United States in particular?

Gorbachev's is an outgoing personality. He fits in easily with almost any company. He doesn't smoke and drinks sparingly. He is conscious of his health and watches his diet. Whenever he can, he tries to get exercise, preferably by walking, something that is not always easy for a man in his position. His curiosity is unbounded, and his questions seem to convey a genuine interest, not just the polite small talk of a distinguished visitor. His personal charm is considerable, enough in fact to lead Prime Minister Margaret Thatcher, never known for her affinity for Communist personalities, to say after their discussions in London, "I like Mr. Gorbachev. We can do business together."[3]

Similarly, Dwayne O. Andreas, the chief executive of a

Midwestern food processing company and the leader of a United States trade group, who met Gorbachev late in 1984 in Moscow, described him as pragmatic, polite, with a good sense of humor, and exceptionally well informed about the United States, even about the nuances of American domestic politics.[4]

And, in the Communist countries of Eastern Europe, Gorbachev is seen as a logical candidate to continue Yuri Andropov's kind of leadership. The present Hungarian regime in particular felt an affinity for Andropov because of his important role in helping place them in power while he was ambassador there. They like the idea that someone trusted by Andropov will be in power in Moscow. "Gorbachev knows Hungary," one official in Budapest told a Western reporter, "and he is interested in our agriculture." Hungary's experiments with decentralization of agriculture are widely believed to have helped inspire similar actions Gorbachev has taken in the Soviet Union, and for that reason he is well regarded in Poland, East Germany, and Bulgaria, which have considered taking similar steps. They look to him as being sympathetic toward the changes that they feel are needed to revitalize their economies.[5]

He is a man of strong opinions, as he displayed occasionally in brief but testy outbursts on his visits to Ottawa and London. In the British capital, for example, in an exchange with a persistent Tory member of Parliament on the touchy issue of human rights, he responded, "I can quote you a few facts about human rights in the United Kingdom. For example, you persecute entire communities, nationalities. You have 2.3 million unemployed. You govern your society. You leave us to govern ours."[6] But he is also a pragmatic man. And that pragmatism seems to have helped him in the domestic politics of the Soviet Union. For example, it is most probable that he

17

was first brought to Moscow at the suggestion of Leonid Brezhnev himself. And in the last months of the Brezhnev regime, he was frequently reported to have been on equally good terms with both Yuri Andropov and Konstantin Chernenko, the principal rivals to succeed Brezhnev as party leader. Indeed, scenarios have been written linking Gorbachev to almost all the senior members of the Politburo from the time he joined their august ranks. He has participated with Foreign Secretary Gromyko in high-level discussions with foreign delegations. On several public occasions he has displayed great camaraderie, if not affection, for Grigory Romanov, the former Leningrad party leader, who frequently was spoken of as a potential rival for power. And like Yuri Andropov, the man who apparently became his patron in the higher reaches of the party, he gives the appearance of being impatient with inefficiency. Like Mikhail Suslov, the ascetic éminence grise who for many years was the chief ideologue of the party—and another of Gorbachev's mentors with a Stavropol background—he is said to abhor the corruption and nepotism that gave rise to Milovan Djilas's New Class of Soviet officialdom. And like both those strong-willed men, he is likely to be ruthless in dealing with transgressors, particularly those who commit economic or political sins. He gave a not too subtle hint of that in a speech in February 1984, when he said there was still a need in the Soviet Union for "enforcing order, being more exacting, organized and disciplined, and waging an uncompromising struggle with negative phenomena that come into conflict with our morals and with socialist legality."[7]

The warning was worthy of Yuri Andropov. In a significant speech in September 1977 marking the centenary of the birth of Feliks Dzerzhinsky, the first Soviet secret police chief, Andropov himself had said, "this does not mean, however, that developed socialist society is guaranteed against the appearance of individuals whose actions are incompatible with either moral or legal norms of Soviet society. The reasons for this are various: political or ideological delusions, religious fanaticism, nationalistic obsessions, resentment caused by personal offense or failures interpreted as the result of underestimation of one's merits and abilities by society, and even mental imbalance in some individuals. All of such cases do occur in our society, a new communist civilization is a complex and difficult process. And it cannot be otherwise."[8]

Gorbachev seems to share his mentor's ideas about dissent, and when, during the leadership of Chernenko, he was entrusted with the ideological fief that Suslov had once held, the policies of the Kremlin seemed to continue as they had in the past. Gorbachev, after all, was trained as a lawyer—a rarity among Soviet leaders—and he brought a lawyer's expertise to deal with the legal administration. However, a Soviet lawyer is bound to have a different view of fair legal procedure than his counterparts in the West. It would therefore be naive to expect Gorbachev to suddenly approve free and open political discussion, for example. That is one area of life in the Soviet Union that is most unlikely to change. But in other ways Gorbachev is a herald of change because he is a man of a new generation in Kremlin politics. And Kremlin politics, like those in the District of Columbia or Westminster, is very much a matter of generations. Thus, where Stalin ruled alone and through fear, Gorbachev and his colleagues act in concert and through compromise. Where Nikita Khrushchev felt powerful enough to initiate his pet projects, such as the dubious scheme to cultivate the so-called Virgin Lands of Central Asia, the political changes in the Soviet Union no longer give the leadership the luxury of such self-indulgence. Gorbachev, too, has radical ideas for changing

Soviet agriculture, but he has had to act much more circum-spectly in having them implemented. Where Leonid Brezh-nev could hold the line, being careful to maintain the status quo, the pressure increasingly is on his successors to produce, to fulfill the promises of a brave new world so long in coming for the average Soviet citizen. During his travels in the West, Gorbachev has displayed great interest in determining the motivations that make workers in factories and on farms so apparently eager to produce more than their counterparts in the Soviet Union. This search for incentives has already been introduced in a limited way in the Soviet Union. With Gorba-chev as the preeminent leader, it is certain to become more prevalent.

In his youth in the Stavropol area, Gorbachev worked dur-ing summer vacations as a harvester operator in the fields. And ever since then, agriculture has been a major preoccupa-tion for him. Indeed, from not long after Kulakov's death in 1978 he has been the man in charge of food production in the Soviet Union. It is therefore reasonable to expect that as Soviet party leader he would continue to give priority to that most daunting of all Moscow's tasks, trying to overcome the vagaries of Russia's relatively brief growing season, the lack of sufficient fertile soil despite the country's huge land mass, and indifference among the rural labor force to make the Soviet Union more nearly self-sufficient in food supply. Gor-bachev has given some indication of being receptive to ideas for innovation in agriculture, particularly in offering incen-tives to farmers and in reducing the emphasis on collective farms that has been the norm since the early 1930s. But up to now, the results must surely have been disappointing to him. Despite greater efforts to produce more domestic meat and despite such imports as New Zealand lamb and Hungarian duck, the average Soviet citizen still finds relatively little meat in the local markets.

While trying to improve agricultural output, Gorbachev will face other strains in the life of the Soviet Union. In the West, the headlines tend to exaggerate the importance of the dissident movement. Most Russians of the 1980s have little feeling for the nuances of democracy as it is known in the West. It is something alien to the Russian tradition, something unknown in the autocratic days of the Romanovs, something unknown since Lenin and Trotsky decided to impose their revolution from above. But within the Communist Party, beneath the surface conformity, the same interest groups that have existed since the death of Stalin can be expected to continue to vie for dominance. It will be Gorbachev's political task to reconcile these competing interests, and it will not be easy. As in the United States, the demands of the military for a greater share of a limited national budget will have to be balanced against the competing demands of the civilian population. The party bureaucracy itself is resistant to change, as was dramatically shown at the end of Yuri Andropov's brief term in office. Although Andropov inveighed against those who resisted change, at his death he was succeeded by Konstantin Chernenko, the archtypical representative of the status quo.

The Soviet Union's new leader will also preside over a nation that in its population makeup is greatly changed from the days of Stalin and is changing still further every year. Although the Russians proper are still the largest individual ethnic component of the population, the multifarious Asian segments of the populace are growing at a much faster rate. This has already caused tensions in the Red Army in Afghanistan and can be expected to do likewise in the Communist Party itself in the coming decades as the Asians become better educated themselves.

Gorbachev's apprenticeship for the Soviet Union's highest office has fitted him unusually well for dealing with foreign policy. More than any other Soviet official in a comparable situation, he has been able to see at firsthand how the other side lives. He knows what the West has to offer in the way of technology and expertise, and he can be expected to pursue them aggressively. If his past career is any guide—and naturally only time can provide the answer—the regime in which he is the dominant figure can be expected to avoid deliberate provocations in favor of peaceful coexistence. He has spoken frequently and favorably of the merits of detente for the Soviet Union and the United States as well as other nations. That is not to say that the Soviet Union is likely to forsake the politically expansionist policies it has pursued for more than six decades. World revolution is more than a slogan to the heirs of Lenin. However, Gorbachev is, of course, first and foremost a Russian despite his Marxist education. And since the earliest days of Muscovy that has meant having a certain suspicion of things foreign—a case of them and us. That would flavor Gorbachev's dealings with the West and with the United States in particular since in the real world the United States is the Soviet Union's rival for supremacy. China, too, occupies a large place in Russian history and the Russian psyche, and it will, of course, occupy a large place in the future policies of the Soviet Union. Negotiations between Moscow and Peking in the latter part of 1984 seemed to indicate that the previous long-standing hostility between the two powers was over and done with. But an accommodation is a long way from friendship.

Gorbachev's road to the top has involved some strange elements. Although he obviously did not arrange it that way, in some ways his progress almost seems to have been a continuous cortege of somber state funerals droning on in the gray expanses of Red Square. After Kulakov's funeral, Gorbachev moved to Moscow and eventually joined the Politburo. After

Suslov's funeral, he took over some of the party organization work. After Brezhnev's funeral, he became obviously more important as perhaps Andropov's key associate. After Andropov's funeral, he became, under Konstantin Chernenko, accepted as "the second general secretary." There were other funerals along the way: Aleksei Kosygin's; Marshal Ustinov's; Arvid Pelshe's. The reasons for that macabre cavalcade are simple. The ruling group had grown older, and for various reasons they clung to power as long as they could. For many Russians, they hung on too long because as they grew older, they also grew more set in their ways, more resistant to change, to initiative, and to progress.

Now it is Gorbachev's turn. Because of the attractiveness of his demeanor, there may be some in the West who will see Gorbachev as more pliable than some of his predecessors. But as he showed in dealing with his sometimes hostile interlocutors in Ottawa and London, Mikhail Gorbachev is not daunted by the outside world. Nor is he likely to be daunted by affairs at home. Self-confident but not arrogant, well-educated, aggressive, well aware of the power he commands and quick to exercise it, the man from Stavropol is a new breed of Soviet leader.

2

The Beginnings in Stavropol

THE NORTHERN Caucasus where Mikhail Sergeyevich Gorbachev was born to a peasant family on March 2, 1931, in the village of Privolnoye, Krasnogvardeisky Region, has always been a place slightly apart from the rest of Russia. It stayed longer under Tatar and Turkish rule. It felt more directly the influences of the non-Russian people of the area where Europe and Asia meet: Armenians, Greeks, Georgians, and so on. It was the area where General Denikin and his White forces made their last stand against the Red Army in 1920, and opposition to the new regime in Moscow continued throughout that decade. And, throughout the 1930s, as Stalin sought to impose collectivization on the unwilling rural peasantry, there was frequent tension in the area that had to be put down by the Cheka.

The peasant opposition was still causing problems for the central government and its representative in Stavropol, a youthful Mikhail Suslov, when Hitler's panzer troops invaded Russia in the summer of 1941. But the arrival of the Germans in the region evoked deeper feelings among the Russian citizens. In regular army units commanded by then Lieut. Gen. Rodion Malinovsky and in partisan bands that Suslov had helped organize for forays behind the enemy lines, the people of the northern Caucasus sought to overthrow the invader. Leonid Brezhnev also took part in the campaign, providing fodder for extensive glorification many years later. Gorbachev would have been a young boy of eleven when the Germans came in 1942 to Stavropol, which was then called Voroshilovsk, after the veteran marshal and crony of Stalin. The Germans occupied the city throughout the autumn and part of the winter. They left on January 21, 1943, forced to do so by the events not so far away in Stalingrad. There, on January 31, von Paulus and the ragged remnant of his army, including twenty-four generals, finally surrendered. The withdrawal of the German troops from the Caucasus included several sharp engagements at places close to young Gorbachev's birthplace, and the passage back and forth of the German and Russian armies had left the countryside in desolation. But the Germans, thanks to the skillful maneuvering of their commander, the panzer general von Kleist, managed to escape the Russian trap and made their way out of the Caucasus to Rostov. Had von Kleist not escaped, the fall of Stalingrad added to the loss of the Germans' Caucasus army would have ended Hitler's ambitions of conquering Russia much earlier than actually happened. Those events and the occupation of his homeland made a deep impression on Gorbachev as they did on all Russians, who still refer to World War II as the Great Patriotic War. Years later, in conversation with a Western official, he recalled traveling by train to Moscow for the first time and being shocked to see the full extent of the damage done to the villages and towns during the war. In the same conversation, he expressed some irritation that the United States and Canada had helped the Western European nations rebuild after the war but that the Soviet Union had had to do its own reconstruction, and for that reason it had taken so much longer to complete.[1]

As things returned to normal, Gorbachev continued his education in the local schools. Life was hard, he would recall, and his family was poor, even by the standards of the area. While he was attending high school, he spent his vacations working on a combine in the local grain fields. Sometimes the harvest ran late into the season, and it was bitterly cold on the primitive Soviet combines—they had no cabs to protect the operator—and young Gorbachev had to wrap himself in straw to try to keep warm.

But, in 1950, all that was to change. He was enrolled in the most prestigious university in all the Soviet Union, Moscow State University, whose sprawling campus and ornate main building that is one of the capital's so-called Stalin skyscrapers are located on the heights across the Moscow River from the Kremlin. At the time Gorbachev entered the university's law school, Stalin was still the autocrat of the Soviet Union. Entrance to all institutions of higher learning was restricted to those with impeccable political backgrounds—whatever that might mean at the time—but in the case of such an eminent institution as Moscow University, matriculation also required unusual academic qualifications, although as one woman who was there at the time recalled, some places were kept open for students representing the various minority races of the Soviet Union, "even though they could barely read Russian."[2] It was also easier sometimes for those with worker or peasant backgrounds to get into the school, and other places were set aside for applicants from the remote areas of the Soviet Union, such as Stavropol. That apparently was how he got into the school. According to two people who knew him at the university, he was sponsored by the Stavropol regional party. His membership in the Komsomol would also have helped.

Although the number of applications would probably have been fewer when Gorbachev was a student, some idea of the exclusivity of the school can be gauged from the fact that in the 1960s, Moscow State each year accepted only 1,900 out of 13,000 applicants.[3] The Law School, thanks to Stalinist era disdain for the spirit—though not the letter—of legal process, was apparently not the best regarded of the university's thirteen faculties. The natural sciences, in the twilight of the Stakanovite era, drew the most applicants, and that may be one reason the young man from rural Stavropol chose to study law, or had it chosen for him.

Not that the Law School did not have a certain prestige when it was needed; professors from the faculty served on state commissions charged with drafting important new legislation.[4] Moreover, in politics an acquaintanceship with legal niceties can be useful in acquiring the right connections.

Even at that age, Gorbachev seems to have been aware of the importance of political connections if he wanted to rise above his provincial background. He quickly became involved as an organizer for the Komsomol at the university and eventually was to become head of the organization at the school. That immediately set him apart since, even in Stalin's time, Komsomol activists tended to be a relatively small minority of the student body; the other students had enough to do to maintain their grades.

People who were at the university at the time remember Gorbachev as an earnest young man overly prone to giving speeches about duty to party and country. "He just loved to make speeches," said one woman who attended the law faculty classes at that time. According to the woman and her husband, also a law student in the early 1950s, Gorbachev was not really interested in the law as such. Even at that time he had set his sights on a career in the party, particularly a career in the party in Moscow.

Disappointment was ahead for him in that regard, however. At the time, the word was that he had been thwarted by someone with superior connections to the party higher-ups. According to this couple, Gorbachev was not a brilliant student, but he was persistent in his ambitions. He knew then what he wanted and went after it with all his ability. They said, too, that despite his Komsomol activity he was not generally known throughout the law school, let alone the university.

The same opinion was offered by another woman who studied in the same building, although not in the Law School. She said that she probably met him in the five years she was there, but she could not remember him at all.[5]

In his position as Komsomol secretary, it seems likely that he made one of the contacts that would serve him well later in life. In the mid-1950s, the first secretary of the Moscow obkom, or district, and the man who supervised Komsomol activities in such a sensitive place as the country's most famous university, was Ivan Kapitonov. Years later, Kapitonov—through his association with Andrei Kirilenko and Leonid Brezhnev—would become a high-ranking Central Committee official overlooking personnel selection and a man in a good position to advance the career of a promising young Komsomol member.[6]

It was about this time that Gorbachev formally joined the Communist Party. It was a significant step because, with his background in the Komsomol and his legal training, it practically made certain that he would have a career in the party administration. Moreover, the party at that juncture was going through a crucial phase of its development. Age was taking its toll of the surviving revolutionary era leaders, and new figures were emerging. (Among them was thirty-eight-year-old Yuri Andropov, a man of growing importance in the Central Committee bureaucracy since 1951.) Also, in the fall of 1952, the first party congress since 1939 was held in Moscow. That it was held at all was a sign that Stalin's powers, though still enormous, were no longer total. It probably would have suited the dictator's purposes if there were no congress, but for the younger men looking to succeed him—Stalin was now 73—it was essential that affairs be put in order before it was too late. However, despite Stalin's apparent wishes that his most obedient servant, Georgi Malenkov, follow in his posts, that was not to be, and when Stalin died in 1953, his eventual successor was Nikita Khrushchev. It was a situation that was to be played over again, with remarkable similarity, two decades later.[7]

In 1955, Gorbachev graduated from law school and returned to his native region, somewhat against his will, but his progress was rapid. In Stavropol, he was given a starting job as deputy chief of a department in the city Komsomol organization. Within a year he was the first secretary of the city Komsomol. That job, too, was to be a stepping-stone to early promotion; by 1958 he had been named initially the second secretary of the regional Komsomol and then the first secretary. He held the latter post until 1962, at which time he was shifted to more serious work, this time as a party organizer of the territorial production administration of collective and state farms. The cycle was complete; the farm boy was back on the farm. But there was a difference; this time he was there as a supervisor of party cadres in the region, not as a combine operator.

Also about this time he was apparently attending evening

classes at the Stavropol Agricultural Institute. Eventually he would graduate in 1967 with a diploma in agronomy, but perhaps more important he had met a student teacher somewhat younger than he was named Raisa. They soon were married.[8]

Advancement continued to be rapid. In 1963, Gorbachev was appointed chief of the agriculture department for the whole Stavropol region. It was an important job for a thirty-two-year-old, and evidently he performed well because in 1966 he was promoted to the sensitive party position of first secretary for the city of Stavropol.

These had been the turbulent Khrushchev years in the Soviet Union. And the turbulence almost certainly turned out to benefit Mikhail Gorbachev's advancement through the ranks of the party.

From 1960, the first party secretary of the Stavropol Region had been Fyodor D. Kulakov, a forty-two-year-old agricultural expert who had once been known as one of Khrushchev's major supporters in his efforts to revolutionize Soviet agriculture. But, somewhere along the way, Kulakov had overstepped the mark and had been demoted from high-ranking republic posts to the relatively obscure regional position in Stavropol, hundreds of miles from Moscow. Even so, he continued to support the leader's call for changes in Soviet farm production, and at a plenum of the Central Committee in March 1962, he said, "Khrushchev is quite right in aiming for a complete reorganization and strengthening of agricultural administration from top to bottom." The words were certainly right for the occasion; but, in subsequent years, indications were to arise that showed Kulakov may have been enthusiastic about farm reforms but he was less enthusiastic about Khrushchev himself.

And Khrushchev's time was up. On Oct. 13, 1964, Khrushchev was on vacation at his dacha at Pitsunda on the Black Sea. That morning he received a visit from a French minister, Gaston Palewski, where they discussed, among other things, whether or not President Charles de Gaulle would seek re-election. Their conversation was interrupted when Khrushchev was summoned to take a telephone call. It was a suggestion that he return to Moscow for a meeting of the Central Committee. Khrushchev demurred, but eventually he was persuaded to go. Accompanied by Anastas Mikoyan, he flew to the capital the next day, only to discover that the majority of his colleagues, led by Mikhail Suslov, were demanding his resignation. After prolonged and heated argument—and a night's respite—Khrushchev resigned. He was succeeded by Leonid Brezhnev.

Brezhnev's origins and past history were to prove especially important for young Mikhail Gorbachev. Brezhnev at this time was just fifty-seven years old, having been born on December 19, 1906, in the small steel town of Kamenskoye, near Dnepropetrovsk in the southern Soviet Union, or Russia as it then was. In his youth he had seen the area ravaged in turn by the German and Russian armies in World War I, the White armies of General Denikin, the guerrillas of Ataman Grigoriev, and the anarchists of Nestor Makhno in the Civil War until, of course, it was eventually subdued by the Red Army.

After some desultory education in various technical schools, Brezhnev had first gone into the Komsomol apparatus, the route to power followed by so many others, including Gorbachev. He was first admitted to the party in 1931, the year of Gorbachev's birth. And by 1938 he shifted from the Komsomol to full-time party duties in the Ukraine, where Nikita Khrushchev had recently been appointed party chief. This was where the so-called Dnieper mafia of close Brezhnev colleagues came together, men like Andrei Kirilenko and Nikolai Shchelokov.

During World War II, Brezhnev served with modest distinction in several areas, including the Caucasus region where Gorbachev was growing up. Then, in 1946 as Khrushchev launched a sweeping purge of Ukrainian party officials, Brezhnev was transferred out of the army to become the party chief in the Zaporozhe Oblast. After serving there for two years, he was shifted again, this time to the Moldavian Republic where lingering nationalist stirrings were causing the Moscow authorities problems. It was in Moldavia that Brezhnev first formed his partnership with Konstantin Chernenko.

From Moldavia, Brezhnev was promoted in 1952—in the last gasp of the Stalin era—to Moscow and candidate membership in the central Presidium. There he again became closely associated with Khrushchev, especially after Stalin's death in 1953, and was chosen the de facto supervisor of Khrushchev's pet Virgin Lands development project. But eventually, as Khrushchev's behavior became more and more erratic, his subordinates plotted a mutiny.

There is no evidence that Brezhnev was among the more active members of the cabal and indeed may have been maneuvered out of the way while it was brewing. However, when Khrushchev was ousted, Brezhnev was promoted into his key office, the general secretaryship.

Brezhnev's new regime realized that in order to cement its grip on power it had to cater to the long-suffering Soviet consumer. Khrushchev had made some moves in that direction, substantial moves when compared to the situation under Stalin. But Brezhnev and his colleagues placed, for the first time, the wishes of the private consumer at the top of their list of priorities. Thus, between 1970 and 1980, the percentage of

Soviet families owning refrigerators rose from 32 percent to 86, the percentage of those owning television sets from 51 to 83, of those owning washing machines from 52 to 70, and of those owning automobiles from 2 to 9.[9]

Against this backdrop then, Gorbachev's career was advancing. In 1968, he was named second secretary of the Stavropol regional party, rising in stature but still on the fringes of real power.

At the center, in 1968, there was another crisis. This one had actually started late in 1967 when Brezhnev had journeyed to Prague to discuss a party problem that had arisen there; the Czechoslovaks wanted to depose their Stalinist party leader, Antonin Novotny. Following the policy that was to be the trademark of his regime, Brezhnev avoided a hard decision. In other words he allowed the Czechoslovaks to make their own decision. That decision was to dump Novotny and to replace him with Alexander Dubcek. What followed in the spring and summer of 1968 was, of course, a sweeping upheaval that threatened briefly to undermine the whole Soviet empire in Eastern Europe. Eventually, the Dubcek regime was squashed by the might of the Red Army and its proxies. But the effect of the so-called Czech spring was to last for years and be felt more than a decade later when troubles arose in Poland.

Although, the Brezhnev regime was having difficulties abroad, at home it was solidifying itself. And one of those most prominent in this process was Fyodor Kulakov. In September 1965, he was elected a secretary of the Central Committee, with special duties in supervising the nation's agriculture. And Gorbachev's promotions followed not far behind. First there had been the Stavropol city appointments, then the shift to the regional party administration as second secretary, and then in 1970 the appointment as first secretary of the Stav-

36

ropol regional party. Mikhail Gorbachev had now arrived on the national scene as one of the country's regional secretaries, the relatively small collection of functionaries who can play— and sometimes have played—crucial roles in deciding who governs the country. Thus, in 1970, Gorbachev was also elected a deputy to the Council of the Union of the Supreme Soviet, the nation's nominal parliament. In addition, he was named a member of the Supreme Soviet's conservation commission, a role fitting a deputy from an area where irrigation and water supplies were important. At the same time, Gorbachev had been awarded his diploma in agronomy.

By this time, Mikhail and Raisa Gorbachev had a baby, a daughter, Irina. Gorbachev was with his political and administrative duties. Raisa was a primary school teacher in Stavropol. They needed help to look after the child and the home; so sympathetic friends helped them find a housekeeper; they were like any other upwardly mobile young couple.[10]

During his term as first secretary in Stavropol, Gorbachev won a reputation as being something of an innovator. One woman who knew him well at this time recalled that there was a small kolkhoz, or collective farm, in the region near Pyatigorsk where he put into practice some of the ideas he had for improving the Soviet Union's outlook on agriculture. He apparently first set about improving the living standards of the people who worked on the collective farm by making provision for installing natural gas and electricity for the dwellings. Then he set aside larger private plots for the collective's members to produce their own food and a surplus for sale to the cities. In addition he persuaded the party and planning authorities to give the collective's members greater freedom over what they produced, when they produced, and even where and for what they sold it. It was a model collective farm and apparently did very well but only because Gorbachev had worked determinedly to make sure it did. "He was very persistent in achieving his goal," said a Stavropol resident of the period.[11]

From all accounts, Gorbachev was unusually popular during his term as party leader in the Stavropol region. One reason for this concerned a drought that afflicted the area in the early 1970s. Most of the collective farmers in the area were convinced that were it not for the quick and helpful arrangements made by Gorbachev, including such things as arranging alternative food supplies for the livestock, there would have been a serious loss of cattle and other animals.[12]

In 1971, Gorbachev was named a member of the party's Central Committee, the sign of his admission to the real ruling cadre. He was now obviously one of the trusted inner circle because, in October the following year, he was sent to Brussels as the head of a delegation to confer with the Communist Party in Belgium, which at that time was important to the Soviet Union because of the Belgians' apparent uncertainty over their allegiance to the North Atlantic Treaty Organization. Then, in 1974, he was elected chairman of the Youth Affairs Commission of the Supreme Soviet. And in May 1975, he went abroad again, this time to West Germany. For the German trip, he was at the head of a fairly prestigious Soviet delegation attending an "anti-Fascist" rally of the German Communist Party marking the thirtieth anniversary of the fall of Hitler. All these positions and journeys were part reward and part signal. The reward was for useful and obedient service, the signal was to the rest of the party that Mikhail Gorbachev was of growing importance in the party.[13]

Arkady N. Shevchenko, a senior representative of the Soviet Union at the United Nations until he defected, remembers meeting Gorbachev about this time while in the

Caucasus for a vacation (according to the former Soviet diplomat it was a popular vacation spot for the top Soviet officials, among them Premier Kosygin and Yuri Andropov, who frequently visited the mineral springs in the region).[14] Shevchenko says that Gorbachev impressed him as being intelligent, well educated, and well mannered. He had earned a reputation as an energetic local party official and as a competent agricultural specialist. And, perhaps most unusual, he was said to be known as a reasonable man, a party apparatchik without the usual arrogance of the species.

Others who knew him at this time agree that he was a pleasant, good-tempered man. One acquaintance remembers, for example, that in about 1974 an American amateur boxing team was touring the area to compete against Russian boxers. Gorbachev attended the bouts and got very excited during close decisions. Other people recall that he was also interested in hockey and soccer scores but in a less enthusiastic manner.

He also was apparently not above using his position to help someone who had helped him in the past. For example, it was well known that he arranged for one of his friends to be named the party secretary in Yessentuki, a resort town near Pyatigorsk that is famous throughout the Soviet Union for its mineral springs and for the mineral water that is bottled there and sold throughout the country. Gorbachev was apparently also well known in Yessentuki and had spent some time there as a Komsomol organizer early in his career.

So life was good. Gorbachev's career seemed to be showing unusual promise. His wife had a career of her own. Their daughter, Irina, was attending a music school and showing promise as a pianist.[15]

During these years, a certain amount of housecleaning was going on in the Kremlin as Leonid Brezhnev consolidated his grip on power. The two principal targets were Nikolai Podgorny and Aleksandr Shelepin, Brezhnev's main rivals. Podgorny was removed from real power when he was elevated to the position of President, a mostly ceremonial role, in December 1965. At the same time Brezhnev moved to pry Shelepin out of his most influential position, as head of the Party-State Control Commission, a watchdog agency that could poke its nose into any department of the party or the government. The commission was abolished, but Shelepin still retained considerable influence in the state security agencies and the Komsomol organization. For several years, this enabled him to maintain some influence, but in January 1975 he was ousted from the Politburo. Aleksei Kosygin had also been a potential rival to Brezhnev, but he gradually retreated to strictly governmental work, and Brezhnev gained full control of the party.[16]

To fill the vacancies being created, Brezhnev was engineering the promotion of many of his close associates from the days when he had been the party chief in Dnepropetrovsk. Most prominent among them were Nikolai Tikhonov and Konstantin Chernenko. But, at the same time, there was a second group rising in the leadership, which while supporting Brezhnev was not wholly in his camp. This might have been called the Suslov wing of the party, and its members included Yuri Andropov, who had been head of the KGB since 1967, and Fyodor Kulakov, who in September 1965 had been named a secretary of the Central Committee with special responsibility for agriculture. And well down the chain of importance, but with access to the top figures, was Mikhail Gorbachev.

If there was need of a sign of his trusted status, it was given in November 1976, when Gorbachev was sent abroad for a third time. This time he was at the head of a delegation of secretaries of major cities and regions invited by the French

Communist Party to visit Paris. It was unusual that a relatively obscure regional party secretary would have been allowed to make three foreign visits in such a short period, let alone act as leader of a delegation. It was a clear signal that Gorbachev had a powerful sponsor or sponsors.

Brezhnev and Suslov had long ago reached an accommodation, and slowly they moved to tidy up the leadership. The final act was the removal of Podgorny from the Politburo in May 1977. By all accounts, Suslov never aspired to the supreme leadership and the ouster of Podgorny from whatever titular power base he had retained meant that Brezhnev was now secure.

But the neat arrangements Brezhnev had made to consolidate his authority were disrupted on July 18, 1978, when Fyodor Kulakov died of a heart attack. His obituary in *Pravda* was signed by Brezhnev and all the other leading figures in the party and the government. Gorbachev's name was there too, immediately following the heads of Central Committee departments.[17]

At the funeral in Red Square three days later, Brezhnev, Kosygin, and Suslov were not present, and the leading mourners were Yuri Andropov, Andrei Gromyko, and A. P. Kirilenko, who delivered the principal eulogy. Mikhail Gorbachev, the young party secretary from Stavropol, spoke too. It was for the most part a pro forma speech, paying proper tribute to Kulakov's worker origins and his devotion to the party of Lenin. But in his peroration, Gorbachev gave a hint of his emotion when he said "Adieu, our friend and comrade." For a brief moment, friendship took precedence over party membership.[18]

In the usual practice of the Soviet Union, various steps were taken to memorialize the nation's loss. Streets in Moscow, Kursk (where Kulakov had been born), Penza, and Stavropol (where he had served) were renamed in Kulakov's honor. Replacing him would not be such a simple matter. At age sixty he had been one of the younger men in a Politburo that was already being called a gerontocracy. The choice of his replacement therefore almost automatically would fall on one of his younger associates. And who was more likely than Mikhail Gorbachev, a protégé not only of Kulakov but a friend of Yuri Andropov and apparently well regarded by the all-important Mikhail Suslov.

In naming some one so relatively young for such a high party and government post the leadership would give the nominee a swift leg up in the Soviet succession ladder. And that would perhaps upset the calculations of some very powerful people, not the least of them Leonid Brezhnev.

3

The
Apprenticeship
in Moscow

IT WAS not long after Fyodor Kulakov's death that Gorbachev was named as his replacement.

The task in front of him was enormous. The Soviet agricultural administration was in the middle of the biggest grain harvest in its history. But severe difficulties were to lie ahead. It was to be the last time for years that the actual harvest exceeded the targets set out in the nation's economic plan. Altogether, 237.4 million tons of grain were gathered in 1978. The following year, the total dropped to 179 million tons, followed by 189 million tons in 1980.

The reasons for the chronic agricultural problems were numerous. The Soviet Union covers an enormous land area, almost two and a half times that of the United States, but much of that vast expanse of territory is inhospitable to agriculture. The climate is harsh—cold and damp in the north, often hot and dry in the south—and, perhaps more important, the area of soil suitable for cereal growing is relatively small. Just a little more than a quarter of Soviet territory can be used at all for agricultural purposes, and only about 10 percent is truly arable. Moreover, suitable combinations of good soil and a moderate and consistent rainfall are frequently difficult to find. The southern areas, such as the fertile "black soil" regions of European Russia and the Stavropol area where Gorbachev grew up, are the most vulnerable to drought, despite extensive use of irrigation.

Another way of looking at the Soviet Union's agriculture problem is to consider latitude. By far the greater part of the Soviet Union lies north of the 49th parallel, which means that most of its regions share a climate comparable to that of northern Canada rather than the United States. Just how far north the Soviet Union is can be judged by realizing that Leningrad is on the same latitude as southern Alaska and Moscow as Hudson Bay, while Tashkent, one of the nation's most southerly cities, is on roughly the same latitude as Chicago. This means that the growing season, although intense, is relatively short, often too short for grains such as wheat.

Russian rulers from the time of the Romanovs have tried to ease the pressure of this economic vise created by bad weather and poor soil. The tsars reached out to colonize new areas of their domains, often by forced migration of the settlers. Their schemes often did not work, and famine was frequent in old Russia. Faced with the economic and agricultural chaos left by World War I, and the revolution and the civil war that followed it, Stalin in the 1930s launched his collectivization program, a scheme that was to bring death to millions, to uproot whole populations, to change the face of Soviet agriculture and rural society but which never did achieve its stated aim of providing a surplus of food for the Russian people.

A new approach was tried under Nikita Khrushchev in the 1950s. The centerpiece of the Khrushchev program was the development of the so-called Virgin Lands of Central Asia.

From the outset, almost everyone except the ebullient Khrushchev recognized the dangers inherent in the program, which sought to till what had been previously exclusively marginal pastoral land in areas where rainfall was often sparse. There were further refinements to the Khrushchev schemes, notably a new concentration on growing maize, even in dry areas. The result was a major economic disaster, and eventually it led to Khrushchev's downfall. Along the way, it had brought Kulakov into direct conflict with Khrushchev and led to his being ousted from his key position as Minister of Cereal Products for the Russian Republic, the largest of the constituent republics of the Soviet Union.

In Stalin's time, Kulakov might well not have been heard of again. But under Khrushchev political punishments were more lenient. Kulakov found himself demoted in 1960 to become first secretary of the party committee in the Stavropol Region, where twenty-nine-year-old Mikhail Gorbachev was a ranking official of the Komsomol.

In the next few years, Gorbachev's rise to prominence would appear to be closely linked to Kulakov's own return to the centers of power.

The crucial events occurred in the summer of 1964. For some time previously, opposition to Khrushchev had apparently been increasing in party circles, particularly among officials concerned with agriculture, among whom Kulakov was prominent. Thus, it was surely not by accident that in September that year Kulakov arranged a hunting and fishing party for several leading Moscow officials on the Manich Lakes in the Stavropol area. It was during this rural retreat, apparently, that the grumbling over Khrushchev's high-handed ways actually developed into concrete plans to unseat him from power.

Khrushchev then went off on vacation himself, to his Black

47

Sea resort, making it easier for his critics to pursue their plans in Moscow. According to one account, the principal figures were Aleksandr Shelepin and Suslov, with the acquiescence of Leonid Brezhnev and Marshal Rodion Malinovsky, the Minister of Defense. By the middle of October, their plans were fully ready, and Brezhnev was appointed to summon Khrushchev to a Central Committee meeting, ostensibly arranged to discuss plans for further reorganization of agriculture. In reality, of course, the meeting to which Khrushchev flew back dealt with agriculture only peripherally, as far as it concerned failures attributed to Khrushchev's ill-fated schemes.

On October 12, 1964, after a prolonged indictment by Suslov for crimes that involved everything from needlessly antagonizing the Chinese to allowing Aleksandr Solzhenitsyn's novels to be published, to his undoubted faults in agriculture, Khrushchev was voted out of office.

Suslov's tirade was just one facet of the attack. Equally strong denunciations came from Dmitri Polyansky, who derided the leader's agricultural policies, and Marshal Malinovsky, who berated Khrushchev's neglect of the military. This was a key change. It was military intervention that had saved Khrushchev earlier; now it would doom him.

Khrushchev's place as First Secretary of the Central Committee was taken by Brezhnev, while Aleksei Kosygin became Chairman of the Council of Ministers. The fortunes of Fyodor Kulakov immediately took a sharp turn for the better, and the career of Mikhail Gorbachev also began to rise above the provincial affairs of the Northern Caucasus.[1]

Gorbachev was distant enough from the center of affairs to avoid the fate of some of the men who had been most prominent in bringing about the downfall of Khrushchev. As

Brezhnev went about the business of consolidating his own grip on ultimate power, a prime target was Aleksandr Shelepin, a former Komsomol wunderkind and head of the KGB who had been a prime mover in Khrushchev's ouster and who probably had higher ambitions of his own. He was shunted aside to a trade union job that effectively was without great influence. Brezhnev also had to deal with Nikolai Podgorny, who like Khrushchev had once been the party chief in the Ukraine and now was apparently threatening to form a coalition with Kosygin at Brezhnev's expense. Overtly the argument was about economic policy and the supremacy of the party—Podgorny and Kosygin were viewed as "reformers" who favored greater emphasis on consumer-oriented production. But in actuality the prize was ultimate power. In the event, Mikhail Suslov came down on Brezhnev's side, and that decided the battle. Brezhnev's two main rivals to the leadership, Podgorny and Shelepin, had been removed. At the same time, however, others apart from Gorbachev were apparently making even more progress in the ascent of the ladders of importance. Yuri Andropov, after playing a key part in the crushing of the Hungarian uprising in 1956, had first been promoted to an important post in charge of the Central Committee department on socialist countries, then to be a secretary of the Central Committee, and eventually to be head of the KGB and a member of the Politburo. Similarly, Konstantin Chernenko had joined the party secretariat and in November 1978 had become a full member of the Politburo.

The death of Kulakov had accelerated Gorbachev's progress, however. On November 27, 1979, he was named a candidate member of the Politburo where, increasingly, two other men with important Stavropol connections, Suslov and Andropov, were real powers. The Brezhnev faction in the leadership, however, was not entirely without influence, and Nikolai Tikhonov, a longtime associate of the general secretary, at this time became a full member of the Politburo.[2]

Gorbachev's new function was generally expected to be as the agricultural specialist in the leadership, but at the session of the Central Committee that elevated him to the Politburo, he played quite a different role. He was appointed head of a committee charged with suggesting changes in the nation's legal apparatus, and he delivered a report outlining new rules for the Supreme Court, the Prosecutor's office, arbitration procedures, and the bar itself. Gorbachev's early training as a lawyer was being put to use, but the incident also provided an insight into his relationship with Suslov, under whose aegis such discussions would normally have been held. And moreover, it was a herald of Gorbachev's own future role as the person in charge of ideological and organizational matters in the leadership.[3]

By this time, both Brezhnev and Kosygin were in failing health. They were increasingly detached from decision-making in key areas. Other elderly members of the Brezhnev Politburo were in similar straits. Arvid Pelshe, the eighty-two-year-old representative of the Baltic republics, was ill, as was Andrei Kirilenko, who had once been viewed as a possible successor to Brezhnev as general secretary of the party. Suslov himself had undergone an operation but was apparently functioning when the crisis in Afghanistan arose.

Afghanistan's geographical location has made it of strategic importance to the Soviet Union since Lenin's time and to tsarist Russia before that; it was not by accident that one of the first foreign treaties signed by the Bolsheviks after they took power was with Kabul.

But as the British had found in the nineteenth century, the Afghans held on to their independence fiercely. In 1973, Moscow had helped engineer the coup that had overthrown the regime of King Zahir and brought Muhammad Daoud to power. Daoud proved so ungrateful for the assistance that he turned against his former allies, the Communists, and early in 1978 he arrested the party leaders and prepared to execute them. But, from their prison cells, the Communists, directed by the party leader, Nur Mohammad Taraki, and his chief aides, Hafizullah Amin and Babrak Karmal, were able to strike back by organizing a countercoup that overthrew Daoud on April 30, 1978.

At that stage, however, the already murky political situation in Afghanistan became even denser. The Soviet authorities, still preferring to try to manipulate events in Kabul from the sidelines rather than become openly and directly involved, had difficulty in deciding which of the several potential leaders to support as the man to take charge. There were three main claimants: Taraki, who may have been Brezhnev's own choice; Amin, who in some reports has been cast as an American agent, and Karmal, who had originally been allied with both Taraki and Amin but later had split with them to form a rival, but still communist, party. At any rate, Taraki emerged as the apparent leader of the new regime, a regime that was quickly perceived by the Afghans as having illegally deposed the rightful ruler, Daoud. In addition, the internecine quarrel between Taraki and Amin, on one hand and Karmal on the other intensified, and Karmal was forced to leave Kabul for a nominal diplomatic assignment in Eastern Europe. Outbreaks of armed opposition to the government continued and general confusion prevailed throughout the country. As the revolt against the Taraki/Amin regime grew in fury, they began to quarrel until on September 16, 1979, Amin ousted Taraki and seized power for himself. Taraki apparently died in a gun battle as Amin's loyalists stormed his official residence. The situation then deteriorated further as Amin waged even more bloody war seeking to crush the noncommunists who wanted Daoud returned to power and had rebelled against the Communists. By December 1979, Moscow seemed to have no choice but to intervene directly to bring stability to its strategic neighbor.

In the swiftly changing situation the reduced-strength Politburo had to decide whether or not to send in the Red Army. The decision to invade, therefore, was apparently made by Andropov, Foreign Minister Andrei Gromyko, Defense Minister Dmitri Ustinov, and Mikhail Gorbachev, even though he was still only an alternate member of the Politburo. The other members, Chernenko, Grishin, and Tikhonov were apparently notified after the fact.

On Christmas Day, five thousand special Soviet troops who had been airlifted in helped storm the presidential palace in Kabul. Within forty-eight hours, they had solved the Amin problem by shooting him and installing a hastily resurrected and repatriated Babrak Karmal as his replacement. But that was not the end of the matter; the resulting civil war for years bogged down large numbers of Red Army personnel and used up huge amounts of Soviet resources, becoming what has been aptly described as Moscow's Vietnam.

Three years later, in his appearance before the parliamentary committees in Ottawa, Gorbachev was quick to offer what the Soviet government obviously regarded as a perfectly reasonable rationale for the invasion. In response to a barely polite question, he said:

> Afghanistan is an old neighbor of ours with whom we have always had friendly relations. In 1978, a people's democratic revolution took place in that country which overturned the feudal regime and chose the course of democratic reform, in

particular, in agriculture and in other areas of social and economic policy. This provoked a sharp reaction on the part of the internal counterrevolutionary forces within the country itself, but the most significant factor was that these forces received widespread support from both Pakistan and Iran, but they primarily received this support by relying on the massive assistance of the Western countries, with the U.S.A. in the forefront, as well as West Germany. China assumed the same position. Generally speaking, by the end of 1979, we had essentially a situation where an undeclared war was being waged against the new regime, against the new order, or against the process that had begun. In this situation the government—incidentally this was not the first nor the last request—there were many—by the end of 1979, the situation was such that war had practically broken out, aimed at nullifying what the people of this neighboring country of ours had won. The Soviet Union responded; and this was not in contravention of any article of the United Nations Charter, by sending a limited contingent of armed forces for one purpose—to render assistance in response to a request made by the legitimate representatives of the people. And these troops are there at the present time. I will tell you right now, to conclude this part of the question, we want to see this problem resolved as soon as possible, resolved by political means, and as you know, definite steps are being taken in that direction at present. . . . Our troops, our soldiers, who are now in that country, and I repeat once more, at the request of the legitimate government, will not remain one day longer once the obstacles to their withdrawal have been removed. What we are talking about here is the cessation of subversive activities against this legally established government. . ."[4]

Gorbachev was carefully following the party line. But,

quite apart from that, the forcefulness of his presentation, the quickness of his thinking, and the seeming reasonableness of his attitude on other questions quite disarmed his Canadian audience, even those diametrically opposed to him ideologically.

It was a bravura performance, but the self-confidence Gorbachev displayed in Ottawa had not been so evident when the Afghanistan crisis first developed. At that time, the mood in Moscow was quite the opposite. In January 1980, President Carter, in response to the Soviet invasion, had imposed an embargo on grain shipments to Russia. The decision was a deep shock to the Soviet authorities since, over the years, they had come to believe that one of the enduring results of detente was the consolidation of the interests of American farmers in maintaining their sizable grain markets in the Soviet Union. Even five years later Gorbachev was to exhibit testiness about American regard for the "sanctity" of contracts. The United States boycott of the Moscow Olympic Games in the same period lacked the economic force of the grain embargo, but its public relations or political effect helped reinforce the effects of the embargo.[5]

Gorbachev was much involved in seeking measures to offset the loss of the American grain, and the resultant activity gave him his first taste of exposure in the national media. Then, in June, *Pravda* gave prominent display to his participation in a conference on the development of power engineering.

At the same time, the situation in Poland went through one of the periodic convulsions that threatened to undermine the Communist regime there. Whereas in the Soviet Union the Orthodox church had become an obedient servant of the state, in Poland the Roman Catholic church had long been a center for opposition to all things Russian, including Marxism-Leninism. The initial disturbances began on July 2, when factory workers in Warsaw and several other areas went on strike to protest increases in meat prices. In the next few days scattered work stoppages occurred throughout the country, until on July 17 the authorities had to call out the army in the southern city of Lublin, where 80,000 workers had called a general strike. The discontent continued to fester throughout the rest of the month until, on August 17, workers in Gdansk and two other northern cities banded together to form an organization that would negotiate for them with the authorities. Solidarity, a labor organization independent of the tame communist labor unions, had been born. At first the government and the party, led by Edward Gierek, refused to deal with Solidarity, but as strikes spread to Warsaw factories and the vital mines of Silesia they were forced to. During the summer and fall, chaos gripped the regime; Communist authority in Warsaw had practically vanished. The Poles and the rest of the world were waiting for the arrival of the Red Army, as had happened in Czechoslovakia and Hungary not so many years before.

But this time, the Soviet actions were much more subtle. Perhaps the lessons of 1956 and 1968 had meant something after all. The preoccupation with Afghanistan was probably another cause for caution. No military commander likes to be involved on two fronts at the same time. At any rate, there was no invasion. Instead, Gierek and most of his associates were dismissed, and in their place there finally emerged a leader capable of resisting Solidarity's demands. He was Gen. Wojciech Jaruzelski, a stern military figure who, it was quickly noted, wore his Russian service decorations in a position of preference over his Polish medals. To a drumbeat of articles and broadcast messages from the Soviet Union, Czechoslovakia, and East Germany about the dangers of counterrevolution, the general reconstituted his government and, by imposing martial law and arresting many of the opposition leaders, gradually diminished the Solidarity threat.

Coupled with the Polish unrest—which created a need for Soviet assistance in maintaining food supplies—and the United States grain embargo, another dismal domestic harvest in 1980 is reported to have led in the Kremlin to some drastic proposals for increasing production.

At the end of October 1980, Brezhnev himself took note of the problem. "Among the questions on which the living standards of the Soviet people depend," he said, "improving the food supply holds first place." He admitted that there were chronic shortages of meat and milk and outlined several ways in which agriculture and life on the farm could be improved. He paid particular attention to the need for improving rural housing but also cited the need for better roads and even better cultural facilities.[6]

Gorbachev was actively promoting his own set of proposals with the same end in mind. Moreover, despite his lack of seniority in the Politburo, by January 1981 he was evidently able to convince his colleagues to endorse the course he advocated. On January 18, the Central Committee issued a decree that to some analysts seemed a step back, at least in rural affairs, to Lenin's New Economic Policy. Under the decree, the existing limits on the use of private land for agriculture were done away with. Although ownership of the land would still reside with the state, the farmers occupying the land could use it for whatever production they wanted. Fully aware that the previously tightly controlled private plots produced an inordinate percentage of milk, meat, eggs, and vegetables, Gorbachev and the others in favor of the new plan were apparently intent on harnessing the farmers' self-interest on a wider scale. They produced solid evidence to back this point of view. In 1982 it was estimated that private-plot farms occupied only 1.4 percent of the Soviet Union's arable land. From that acreage, however, came 61 percent of the nation's potatoes, 54 percent of its fruit, 34 percent of its eggs, 30 percent of its vegetables, and 29 percent of the meat and milk.[7]

Several other refinements to the new plan also doubtless raised opposition among some party leaders. The effect of the first such refinement meant that livestock produced under the new scheme could be sold to the state at a negotiable price. In other words, the existing fixed price system was being abandoned, at least in part. By a second provision, the USSR State Bank was told to provide financing for the holders of the private plots on unusually easy credit.

The debate over how to handle the private plots had been going on for some time. The Soviet press had printed numerous articles giving both sides of the dispute. In one such article, a party official from the Dnieper River bottomlands complained that when harvest time came on the local collective farms, hundreds of the men and women who should have been helping were "far away selling tomatoes, cucumbers, and various other vegetables." He gave some idea of the scope of the private production: "Over five thousand permanent greenhouses, with boilers and electric heaters, have been built in the district without proper authorization. . . . An irrigation network has been developed for vegetable gardens; more than eight thousand wells have been drilled. . . . High-powered pumps hum from morning to night. Instead of housing livestock, almost everyone's shed is filled with fertilizer, herbicides, and other chemical agents." He added that five thousand able-bodied persons in the district did not take part in the work of the collective farms, but concentrated instead on their own plots. This created serious difficulties when harvest and planting time came around.[8]

However, the same issue of *Pravda* carried a cautionary article by an academic suggesting that although there were some bad things about the private plots, they should be better developed and not done away with. "Support for personal farming is now an important part of the CPSU's agrarian policy," he said.

But Gorbachev's proposals apparently went too far. Had the proposed changes been maintained, the face of Soviet agriculture would have been drastically altered. However, on April 1, 1981, President Reagan revoked the American grain embargo. The pressure for immediate change was removed in the Soviet Union, and the drastic revisions of agricultural policy were quickly canceled.[9]

The episode is interesting quite apart from the light it sheds on the difficulties facing the Soviet regime in trying to improve agricultural output. It also helps illustrate the divided nature of the Soviet leadership in the waning days of the Brezhnev regime, divisions that persisted through the short term of Yuri Andropov and into that of Konstantin Chernenko as the party's First Secretary. The ages of the men around Brezhnev and his immediate successors created one obvious difference, but much more important was the difference in attitude and outlook. Brezhnev, Kosygin, Suslov, Tikhonov, Chernenko, and others had been matured in the time of Stalin, had been old enough to hold responsible positions in World War II, and had endured the hurly-burly Khrushchev period. The events, momentous and mundane, that they had witnessed shaped their whole outlook. That helps explain why Brezhnev can be seen as such a patient striver for maintaining the status quo.

Andropov seems to have been somewhat apart from this group. And the reasons for the separation are difficult to assess, except for the obvious ambition he displayed and his lack of the shared backgrounds of Brezhnev, Chernenko, and some of the others in the so-called Dnieper mafia. Gorbachev was also an outsider although he and Andropov had been friends for some years.

Their commonality of interests was doubtless heightened by the changes that were beginning to be necessary in the Soviet leadership. For some time, Aleksei Kosygin had been in obviously poor health and finally, in October 1980, he resigned as Prime Minister. At one time, Kosygin had been a serious contender for the highest offices in the party and the regime, but eventually Brezhnev had surpassed him, and Kosygin became the personification of the supreme bureaucrat, a man apart from the party struggles. He was to live only a couple more months, dying on December 18. His departure gave Brezhnev a further opportunity to reinforce the group in office around him. The new Prime Minister was Nikolai Tikhonov, one of the aging Dnepropetrovsk cronies.

The ensuing changes also were important to Gorbachev. On October 22, 1980, at the age of forty-nine, he was named a full member of the Politburo. His rise to such eminence had been unusually rapid; it had been only a year since he had first become a candidate member of the top ruling body of the Soviet Union. And the rapidity of his advancement was already giving rise to speculation that Gorbachev was a possible successor to Brezhnev as the ultimate leader.

Gorbachev at this stage was still a long way from supreme power, but he was cementing relationships that would help him toward that end. As the events preceding the invasion of Afghanistan had shown, power in Moscow increasingly had gravitated to Suslov and Andropov, the two most active and most senior members of the ruling group. Suslov was also aging and in indifferent health, but he still managed to keep his grip on the party, ideologically and organizationally.

Andropov, from his powerful base as head of the KGB, was able to influence policy both domestically and in foreign affairs. Both were in positions to help advance Gorbachev's career, and in the next few years they did. Thus, on Gorbachev's fiftieth birthday, March 1, 1981, he was awarded the Order of Lenin "for great services to the party and the state."

In the waning months of 1980 and the beginning of 1981, Andropov was apparently moving to ensure his own promotion. To do that meant having to undermine Brezhnev's already weak power structure. Of course, no one outside the Kremlin can say with certainty what actually happened or who conspired to bring it about, but there are obvious signs that Brezhnev's opponents, or critics, moved against him in several ways.

The first came to light on the occasion of the leader's seventy-fifth birthday, on December 19, 1981. As had been the custom in recent years, the birthday was an excuse for adulation of the most sycophantic nature. In 1981, the most unusual aspect of this was the presence in Moscow of Afghanistan's President Babrak Karmal, who presented a tearful Brezhnev with the Afghan Order of Freedom.

In Leningrad, the venerable elder's birthday was being noted in a quite different and less effusive manner. In the old capital the literary-political journal *Aurora* offered its own tribute. The magazine is named for the cruiser *Aurora*, now docked harmlessly on the banks of the Neva, but best known for the shots it fired at the nearby Winter Palace during the October Revolution in 1917. Now the magazine *Aurora* was firing a few shots of its own at another venerable structure. On the cover of the December issue was Brezhnev's portrait. But inside was an obvious lampoon of the geriatric leader, including—appropriately on page 75—a politically blasphemous "Birthday Speech." One striking segment of the material dealt caustically and obviously with the frequent reports of Brezhnev's imminent death:

> The day before yesterday I heard that he had died, and I freely admit that I was filled with joy and pride. But my joy was premature. I hope, however, that we won't have to wait for long. He won't disappoint us. We all believe in him so! Let's hope that he completes the work he still has in hand, and gladdens our hearts as soon as possible.[10]

In Stalin's Russia, the mere writing of such a lampoon, let alone its publication, would have been cause for a death sentence. Even in the less autocratic Khrushchev period, or earlier in the Brezhnev regime, the punishment for such an offense would have been harsh. But on this occasion, the penalties were mild, so mild in fact that it was obvious that the whole incident had approval at a high level. And all the indications are that the high level reached to the leadership of the KGB.

Within a few weeks, further events were to shake the Soviet leadership and illustrate even more vividly how tenuous Brezhnev's hold on power had become.

But first, the aging power structure in Moscow was disturbed by the death of seventy-nine-year-old Mikhail Suslov, that seemingly eternal symbol of communist rectitude. According to the official account, Suslov had suffered a stroke on January 21, 1982, and his condition had worsened until he died a week later. His funeral was unusually ostentatious, even for the spectacles of that kind to which the Soviet regime is prone. In the biting cold made worse by the raised and exposed expanse of Red Square, an enfeebled Leonid Brezhnev led the mourners in what was described as the most elaborate such ceremony since the death of Stalin. "Sleep in

peace, our dear friend," mumbled Brezhnev as the full Politburo gathered atop the Lenin Mausoleum. "You lived a great
and glorious life, you did much for the party and the people,
and they will maintain your bright memory." Suslov's body
had lain in state in the ornate House of Unions in Central
Moscow, where Lenin and Stalin had also been mourned. His
body was brought to Red Square on a gun carriage towed by
an armored car and accompanied by a band playing Chopin's
"Funeral March." Suslov was buried alongside Stalin, between the mausoleum and the red brick Kremlin wall in a row
of graves reserved for the party's most illustrious figures.
Besides Stalin the row includes Felix Dzerzhinsky, the first
secret police chief; Mikhail Frunze, a civil war hero and
military leader; Marshal Klementi Voroshilov, another long-
time military figure and drinking crony of the aging Stalin;
and others of similar stature.[11]

Suslov's death immediately set in motion a more or less
open contest between Chernenko and Andropov for the key
departments that Suslov had supervised. Even though Gorbachev was not directly involved in this struggle—he had
enough to cope with in agriculture—he was to be greatly
affected by the outcome.

Authoritative analysts suggest that there was a definite rift
in the Politburo over who should succeed to Suslov's eminent
domain. It is generally believed that Brezhnev and his coterie
favored Chernenko, while Defense Minister Ustinov, Vladimir Shcherbitsky, and some others wanted Andropov to be
named. While the Politburo hesitated about making a decision, Brezhnev remained in Moscow throughout the late winter instead of taking his usual vacation in Sochi. But, apparently as an opportunity to get at least a little sun, he flew to
Tashkent, capital of the Uzbek Republic, to present the
republic with an Order of Lenin, marking the sixtieth anni-

versary of the founding of the USSR. The trip would also have served to show how healthy Brezhnev was, thus refuting the ever-present rumors of his imminent demise. To help promote this part of the journey, his departure from Tashkent was given extensive television coverage, and more television crews were waiting in Moscow to record his triumphant return to the capital. But en route, Brezhnev suffered a stroke and had to be carried off the plane in a stretcher and rushed to a Kremlin hospital. For weeks, the old man lost the ability to speak and indeed was apparently close to death.[12]

In the interval, Andropov moved to consolidate his grip on Suslov's former empire. And indeed he was much more qualified for the role than was Chernenko. Andropov had worked under Suslov's direction in the Central Committee apparatus that dealt with foreign regimes from 1957 to 1967, and at the KGB he had dealt extensively with Suslov.

Brezhnev had recovered sufficiently by the end of May 1982, to attend the Politburo meeting at which the decision was made to move Andropov to the Secretariat and to bring ideological matters under his jurisdiction. All indications are that the discussion was heated; the meeting lasted no less than six hours. But in the end Andropov won, and the Brezhnev forces suffered a serious setback.

Nor was that their only reverse. Other events were also in progress that were perhaps even more important in illustrating how Brezhnev's authority had been discredited. The first incident had occurred on January 19, 1982, when Gen. Semyon Tsvigun, Brezhnev's wife's brother-in-law and also Andropov's deputy at the KGB, was found dead of a gunshot wound in his office. That apparently set in motion a series of arrests that raised the specter of an embezzlement scandal directly at Brezhnev's door. On January 29, the day of the Suslov obsequies, Boris Buryatia, a high-living Bolshoi Opera singer, was arrested. A search of his apartment reportedly revealed a stash of diamonds, which Buryatia said did not belong to him but were the property of his lover, Galina Churbanova. Mrs. Churbanova's husband, Lieut. Gen. Yuri Churbanov, was the first deputy minister in charge of the MVD, the domestic security agency, but even more important, her father was Leonid Brezhnev himself. Then, Anatoly Kolevatov, the director of the State Circus, was arrested and told a similar tale about the cache belonging to Mrs. Churbanova when $200,000 in hard currency and $1 million worth of diamonds were found in his apartment.[13]

Exactly how the Tsvigun suicide—if that is what it was—meshed into the other incidents has never been clarified although there have been all sorts of rumors involving anti-Brezhnev plots and even murder, but the combination of scandal and the Brezhnev family could only further erode the aging leader's authority. When coupled with the death of Mikhail Suslov, the incidents increased the stature of Yuri Andropov and lessened the immediate succession hopes of Konstantin Chernenko, Brezhnev's long-time crony. Indeed, some analysts suggest that from the spring of 1982 Andropov was the de facto leader of the Soviet Union.

That had not been apparent immediately after the death of Suslov. At that time it had seemed that Chernenko had assumed Suslov's key role as spokesman for the leadership on ideological and party affairs. But in the spring, Brezhnev's illness had enabled Andropov to outflank Chernenko. The decision to shift Andropov from the KGB to the central party secretariat, first taken at the stormy Politburo session, was officially announced to a party plenum in late May. In the Politburo, Chernenko was apparently supported only by a fragile Brezhnev, for whom he had acted as a sort of personal manager. Even the Brezhnev loyalists on the Politburo—

Dinmukhammed Kunaev and Vladimir Shcherbitsky—objected to the elevation of Chernenko, whom they regarded as their junior since he had been raised to the Politburo rank long after they had. Foreign Minister Gromyko and Defense Minister Ustinov also objected to Chernenko, and Mikhail Gorbachev favored his friend Andropov. Ability doesn't seem to have entered into the debate; if it had by all accounts Chernenko would have been an instant loser.[14]

Andropov was a figure of stern probity, as he had made clear in a speech given in Moscow on April 22 to mark the 112th anniversary of Lenin's birth.

After stating the usual line that life in the Soviet Union was improving every day in every way, he said:

> But this does not mean that we are totally free of shortcomings and problems, of phenomena against which consistent and resolute struggle must be waged. For example, cases of embezzlement, bribery, red tape, lack of respect for the individual, and other antisocial phenomena still do come up—and cause legitimate revulsion among the Soviet people. And it doesn't really matter whether they have come down to us from the past or are brought in from abroad by parasites who batten on certain shortcomings in our development. If such phenomena do exist, they stand in our way; and it is the duty of each Communist—and each citizen, one might add—to battle against them. The Soviet people fully support the measures which the party takes to eradicate them.[15]

Brezhnev, who was in the audience, and some of his close colleagues who knew of the recent scandals must have winced at the implied threat.

As Andropov's stature had grown, his friend Mikhail Gorbachev's authority had increased too. Along with Andropov and Chernenko, Gorbachev was now one of three men who simultaneously held seats on the Politburo and were national party secretaries, a combination necessary for ultimate power in the Soviet Union.

But Gorbachev was having problems, too. As the man responsible for agriculture, the continued bad news on that aspect of the economy could only adversely affect his standing in the regime. The introduction of a new food program, promised by Brezhnev, was postponed until the end of May 1982. Gorbachev set out on an inspection tour of the main farming areas where, following a bad spring, there were already signs of drought in several regions.[16]

For the moment, however, Andropov was in the ascendant. And the campaign, generally attributed to him, against Brezhnev continued apace. Soon after the Plenum of the Central Committee late in May, Brezhnev apparently left for his dacha in the Crimea. Andropov was now in full charge of the party secretariat, and he took full advantage of that position.

The immediate target was a long-time Brezhnev crony, Sergei Medunov, the party secretary of the Krasnodar Region, in which was situated the resort center of Sochi. Stalin had once had a dacha there and many leading Soviet figures still spent their summers in Sochi.

Gorbachev may well have played a leading part in helping Andropov bring about the downfall of Medunov. In one version of the affair, it is stated that in previous years Andropov had made a practice each summer of returning to the Stavropol area where he had been born to spend vacations at Krasnye Kamni, a sanitorium for the party higher-ups. When he did so, he was met at the airport, according to protocol, by the local party secretary, Mikhail Gorbachev. In this way, the friendship between the two men developed and in 1978 Gorbachev confided in Andropov about the misdeeds of his neighboring official, Medunov. The two regional secretaries inevitably saw themselves as competitors, and Gorbachev is said to have complained that Medunov achieved his successes by permitting corrupt practices, which he got away with because he was being protected by Brezhnev. Gorbachev is said to have collected a dossier of the offenses committed in the Krasnodar Region, detailing how it was necessary to pay bribes to buy a car, get an apartment, a job, or even a hotel room. Andropov is said to then have organized a campaign by which irate area residents complained in letters to the Central Committee and to the KGB about the goings on in and around Sochi. Finally, *Pravda* itself printed some of the letters, but Medunov survived unscathed, and the editors who had published the offending letters were apparently reprimanded. Andropov then is said to have tried more direct tactics, having the local prosecutor seek to indict some of the offenders. Again he failed; the prosecutor was removed from office, while Medunov stayed put. Moreover, Vitaly Vorotnikov, a deputy premier of the Russian Republic—and nominally Medunov's boss—who had supported the anti-Medunov campaign, was removed from office and sent to Cuba as ambassador. Andropov persisted and, in 1980, the mayor of Sochi was convicted of corruption and sentenced to thirteen years in prison. Again, however, Brezhnev protected Medunov. The passage of two years and Brezhnev's increasing incapacity changed that. In July 1982, *Pravda* printed a brief item saying that Medunov had been relieved of his post and had been "transferred to other work." To replace him, Vitaly Vorotnikov was recalled from Cuba.[17]

Brezhnev may have been out of the picture, but Chernenko apparently was still trying to outdo Andropov in the contest for the succession. Some of the skirmishing was petty in the extreme. Chernenko factionalists, for example, began to spread rumors that Andropov was not of pure Russian ancestry and therefore lacked what since Stalin has generally been regarded as an essential requirement for the ultimate leadership. Some rumors made him part Armenian, others made him a quarter Jewish. In fact, given the probable language root of his name, his ancestors most likely were Russified Greeks.[18]

While this was going on, the elderly Brezhnev was enjoying the sun in the south. Late in the summer, he traveled to Baku in Azerbaijan where, apparently to demonstrate his rejuvenation, he was to give a speech that would be telecast live. Brezhnev began reading the speech and continued doing so for about ten minutes. At that stage an aide appeared beside him, whisked away the copy of the speech that Brezhnev had been reading and replaced it with another. Brezhnev looked stunned, then stammered, "It was not my fault. I have to start all over again." The live broadcast ended there, with the second speech being read by an announcer. Later events, including the promotion—and not the punishment—of the aide who had changed the speeches, clearly suggest that the whole affair was prearranged, probably by Yuri Andropov.[19]

Throughout the fall there were continual reports that Brezhnev was again dead or dying. But late in the autumn he began to show signs of increasing activity. The intention may well have been to help push forward the succession chances of Chernenko and the long-time Brezhnev colleagues who were ranked behind him. Thus, on November 2, 1982, Brezhnev conferred the Order of Lenin and a second gold medal of the Hero of Socialist Labor on Tikhonov. Brezhnev's statement on the occasion, which seemed to have been chosen at random and not for any commemorative purpose, was full of the code phrases that carry special significance in Kremlinology. Brezhnev said that Tikhonov had "rich experience," had performed "uncommon hard work," had shown "selflessness in labor," and most important of all, "I have known him well for many a decade." It was an obvious endorsement for being continued in his leading role in the party and the regime.[20] Then, on November 7, at the annual commemoration in Red Square of the 1917 Bolshevik Revolution, Brezhnev appeared in public again. Although he was obviously in frail health, had to be assisted by two aides, and had to pause on every step as he mounted the rostrum, he remained for three hours atop the Lenin Mausoleum, exposed to the bitter chill of a Moscow autumn while the parade marched past. He wore a heavy overcoat and a fur hat and tinted sunglasses to lessen the sun's glare, but Westerners and Russians alike were surprised that he had been put through what was obviously an ordeal. And then, after the parade he had spoken at a reception in the Kremlin for the diplomatic corps. It was a trying day for the old man.[21]

Three days later, after having breakfasted with his wife, Viktoria, at their apartment on Kutuzovsky Prospekt, and having read *Pravda* for a while, he arose from the table and went into his bedroom. When he did not appear for some time, Mrs. Brezhnev went to see what he was doing. She found him sprawled on the floor, dead.

The official announcement, intoned simultaneously by somber announcers on radio and television said:

> The Central Committee of the Communist Party of the Soviet Union, the Presidium of the USSR Supreme Soviet, and the Council of Ministers of the USSR inform with deep sorrow the party and the entire Soviet people that Leonid Ilyich Brezhnev, general secretary of the CPSU Central Committee and president of the Presidium of the USSR Supreme Soviet, died a sudden death at 8:30 A.M. on November 10, 1982.
>
> The name of Leonid Ilyich Brezhnev, a true continuer of Lenin's great cause and an ardent champion of peace and

Communism, will live forever in the hearts of the Soviet people and the entire progressive mankind.

Brezhnev's funeral was staged with the full panoply of ceremonial with which the Soviet endows such events. The coffin was borne on a gun carriage from the House of Unions the half mile to the Lenin Mausoleum in Red Square. In front of the coffin were dozens of senior military officers carrying a massive portrait of the dead leader. Behind them came more officers bearing the dozens of funeral wreaths. Then came forty-two colonels each bearing a red satin cushion with Brezhnev's medals and decorations. Then came the coffin and its honor guard of nattily dressed young soldiers. Behind them were the family, including his widow, Viktoria, and his daughter, Galina, with her husband, then the Politburo led by Andropov and then hundreds of lesser officials. As bands played Chopin's "Funeral March," the cortege took forty-five minutes to complete its journey. Then, with the open coffin resting in front of him, Andropov delivered the eulogy. He praised the dead leader as "flesh of the flesh and bone of the bone of the people," and called him "a worker and soldier, an outstanding organizer and a wise political leader." Defense Minister Ustinov also spoke, but Konstantin Chernenko, Brezhnev's closest aide and generally believed to have been his choice as successor, did not speak. At one stage of the ceremony, Chernenko had been squeezed into a space behind Andropov in the crush at the graveside. Noticing this, Andropov reached back and gestured for Chernenko to move forward.[22]

The usual public ritual was being played out. But, in the privacy of the Kremlin, other matters were afoot.

4

In the
Shadow of
Andropov

ON NOVEMBER 12, 1982, members of the Central Committee of the Communist Party began to gather in Moscow for the plenum at which they would officially select the new General Secretary to replace Brezhnev. There was some apprehension, it is said, among the committee members, particularly among those who held bureaucratic positions largely because of their association with the dead leader. The recent dismissal of Medunov from his post in Krasnodar was a warning not unnoticed.

In actual fact, the choice of the new leader had been made on the day that Brezhnev had died. At 4 P.M. that day, when all efforts to revive the stricken man had obviously failed, a special session of an enlarged Politburo was summoned. In addition to the full members and candidate members, the Marshals of the Soviet Union were also present. The chairman was Vladimir Shcherbitsky, the Ukrainian party secretary. Almost immediately, Marshal Ustinov—in addition to his post as Defense Minister, he was also a full voting member of the Politburo—proposed the nomination of Yuri Andropov to the post of general secretary. That left no doubt as to where the military stood. Foreign Secretary Andrei Gromyko apparently also indicated his approval of the nomination. Viktor Grishin, on behalf of the Moscow regional party, and Grigory Romanov, speaking for the Leningrad party, also sided with Andropov. Although Gorbachev had ties to the Chernenko camp and some accounts of what transpired at the meeting have him abstaining from voting, it seems certain that he sided with his friend and patron, Andropov. Two Politburo members, the aging and ailing Kirilenko and Pelshe, were absent. Konstantin Chernenko is said to have realized immediately that he did not have the votes to oppose the nomination, and so it was quickly approved.[1]

There really had been no other choice. It is an unwritten requirement for election to the ultimate leadership, and a political necessity, that the candidates not only be members of the Politburo but also hold ranking positions in the Secretariat, the core of the party administration. At the time of Brezhnev's death, four people held such dual posts. Kirilenko, who was too old and too ill to be a serious candidate. Gorbachev, who was still too much of a newcomer. Chernenko, whose principal credential was that he was Brezhnev's chief aide de camp. And Andropov, the one man among them with considerable administrative experience, with extensive knowledge of foreign policy, and with the correct ideological background.

Andropov at this time was sixty-eight, having been born on June 15, 1914, in the village of Nagutskaya in Stavropol Province where his father was a railroad employee. As a young man he worked as a telegraph operator and as a boatman on the Volga. From a young age, however, he had also been involved in Komsomol activities, and after graduating from a technical college in Rybinsk, near Yaroslavl, in 1936 he went into full-time Komsomol work. That took him, in 1940, to the new Karelo-Finnish Republic wrested from Finland in the 1939-40 Winter War and later renamed the Karelian Autonomous Republic. Andropov and his colleagues were charged with sovietizing the sometimes rebellious citizenry, many of whom eventually were allowed to migrate to Finland. In 1944, Andropov had transferred into party work, and by 1947 was the republic's second secretary under the well-known Bolshevik Otto Kuusinen. It was apparently with Kuusinen's sponsorship that Andropov took his next step up the party ladder, in 1951, when he moved into the Central Committee Secretariat. Two years later he was shifted to the diplomatic service, being posted to Hungary where in 1954 he became ambassador. His service there proved crucial. He played a key role in crushing the 1956 Hungarian uprising, and a year later Andropov was brought back to Moscow to head the Central Committee's foreign affairs department. He continued working in this area through the tumultuous events surrounding the fall of Khrushchev and the promotion of Brezhnev to the leadership. In 1967 he was named head of the KGB, a position he was to hold for fifteen years. He had been named to the Politburo a month after the KGB appointment. Then, following Suslov's death he had moved back to the secretariat with overall charge of ideological and personnel matters, a key position from which to secure the supreme leadership.

Thus, when it came to the plenum, the delegates, some of whom might have been justifiably fearful of an Andropov succession, found that they had little option but to go along with the Politburo's decision. In a break with the usual procedure, the presiding officer was Andropov, who apparently opened the meeting with a short speech. He then called on

Chernenko to deliver a report from the Politburo on the succession, a clear signal to the delegates on the way they were to act. Chernenko went along with the wishes of the Politburo majority and placed Andropov's name in nomination, but there were signs that he was not happy with the task. In his address he described himself—and not Andropov as might have been expected—as having been privileged "to be at the side of Leonid Ilyich, to listen to him personally, to feel his mental acuteness, his resourcefulness and liveliness." And then, perhaps most importantly, he went on to remind Andropov that it was essential that the collective leadership that had marked the later Brezhnev years had to be continued. "Today it is twice, three times as important to conduct business in the party collectively," he said.[2]

But the Soviet public had its own idea of how collective the Andropov leadership would be. Almost immediately after his election a joke began to circulate in Moscow. In it, a foreign journalist is said to have asked Andropov how he could be sure that the people would follow him. "Aha," said Andropov, "of course they will follow me. And those who don't will follow Brezhnev."[3]

Indeed, from the very beginning of his term in office, Andropov moved swiftly to effect changes. Kirilenko's de facto removal from the Politburo was made official within a month. Pelshe was allowed to remain, but it was obvious that age and illness would soon remove him too. Andropov moved in other ways as well. It was almost as if he knew that his time was short. For example, he assumed the post of President in June 1983, just six months after becoming the general secretary. Brezhnev had taken more than a decade to achieve that largely symbolic but important dual ranking.

The most striking example of how things had changed occurred one Friday afternoon at the tool factory outside

Moscow, named for the great revolutionary figure Sergo Ordzhonikidze. As the workers toiled at their places, suddenly their routine was interrupted by a group of officials, accompanying a tall, but slightly stooped graying man of obvious importance. As the party walked along, he would stop and talk to the workers asking them about comparative wage scales, about their families, about whether or not the plant sent assistance to other communist countries. He even found occasion to joke—or was he joking?—about the hypocrisy indulged in in setting and revising the production targets under the various plans. Andropov, for the unusual visitor was indeed the new general secretary, then spoke impromptu to the assembled workers.

> Everything we do and produce must be done and produced, as far as possible, at minimum cost and high quality, quickly and durably. We must produce more goods to fill the shelves. ... Miracles, as they say, don't happen. You understand that the government can only provide as many goods as are produced. A wage increase cannot provide a real improvement in the standard of living, unless it goes together with a better supply of good-quality products which people want and unless services improve.

Such exhortations had been made before, but the workers at the Ordzhonikidze plant, and the wider audience that soon heard of the visit, could sense that there was a new attitude being exhibited by the new leader. And if they were in any doubt, they soon got an unmistakable message when Andropov said: "Comrades, I'd like you to understand me correctly. Strengthening discipline is not just an issue for workers or engineers and technicians. It applies to everyone, starting with ministers."[4]

He had sounded the same note in his first major policy address as general secretary, delivered to a Central Committee plenum on November 22, 1982. Speaking of the difficulties in meeting the budget and fulfilling the latest five-year plan, Andropov said:

> The principal indicator of the economy's effectiveness—labor productivity—is growing at a rate which cannot satisfy us. Inconsistency is still a problem in the development of the raw materials and processing industries. The material intensiveness of production is not being practically lowered.
>
> As before, plans are being fulfilled at the cost of tremendous input and production expenses. There are still quite a few economic managers who, willingly citing the oft-cited words of Leonid Ilyich that the economy must be economical, do little in practice to make it so.
>
> Evidently, the force of inertia and old habits still have their effect. And perhaps some people simply do not know how to tackle the job.... Conditions have to be provided—both economic and organizational—that will stimulate productive work, initiative, and enterprise. And, conversely, poor work, inaction, and irresponsibility will have to tell in the most direct and inexorable way on the material remuneration, service status, and moral prestige of workers."[5]

These were strong words, and the actions that preceded them seemed to imply that the laissez-faire days of the Brezhnev era were gone for good. By and large, the Russian people were pleased, despite Andropov's tough reputation as head of the KGB. Moreover, ironically enough, there were many similarities between Andropov and the men who had preceded him in the general secretary's position. Like Khrushchev and Brezhnev he was a real apparatchik, a creature of the bureaucracy. Also like them, he was a man of relatively little formal education. And finally, like them he was willing to put the interests of the party and the state above all else, as was shown by his performance in Hungary and in his years as head of the KGB, the longest term in that office in Soviet history.[6]

The most visible sign of Andropov's drive for discipline in the economy was to order the police to round up workers playing hookey from their jobs. This campaign began less than a month after Andropov took charge when the Politburo announced that it had discussed workers' letters that had urged tighter discipline in the workplace. Simultaneously the party press began to print similar missives and the main evening news program on television, "Vremya," aired clips of workers voicing complaints about drunkenness on the job, chronic lateness on the part of some employees, and so on. Then, in January, special party cadres were assigned to raid movie houses, sports events, public baths, and especially lines for hard-to-come-by food items in search of people ducking out from work. To offset possible complaints about the inability of some workers to get to the shops, the stores were told to stay open later so that all would have the opportunity to get what they needed. In addition, some large plants were told to open such conveniences as shoe repair shops to help their workers avoid having to lose work time.[7]

The drive for efficiency was moving in other directions too, one of which must have been most unnerving to the comfortable Brezhnev-era appointees. Within a week of taking office, Andropov had begun what can only be described as a purge of middle-ranking officials of dubious reputations. One of the first to go was Ivan Pavlovsky, the minister in charge of the chronically inefficient railroad system. Less surprising, given Andropov's reputation for personal rectitude, was the firing of Nikolai Shchelokov, a long-time Brezhnev ally but also a man with a reputation for turning a blind eye to official transgressions. An interesting sidelight to Shchelokov's departure was an obviously orchestrated press campaign about street crime problems, a direct reflection on the militsia over which Shchelokov had responsibility. Such was the intensity of the program of denigration that Shchelokov's wife is reported to have committed suicide during the investigation into her husband's affairs. Some of the men who were ousted in the next few weeks were of retirement age anyway, but many of them were Brezhnev colleagues and supporters of long standing and probably would have kept their positions as long as they could totter into the office, had not their patron died. Others, of course, were known for their corrupt ways. It was as if Andropov had two objectives: to get rid of the decrepit and the decadent and to bring new vigor to the administration.[8]

Gorbachev, as a member of the Politburo, would almost certainly have had a general say in the firings, and he may have been directly involved in some of them since they involved officials in areas such as consumer-oriented industry, where he was increasingly becoming involved.

It was much clearer where Gorbachev's influence was directly felt early in the Andropov regime. In agriculture under Brezhnev, the policy generally had been to try to do more in a bigger way. That was one reason why the radical plan to stimulate production in January 1981 had been undermined. Under Andropov—and at Gorbachev's suggestion—once again there was to be much more attention to providing incentives for increased production. Therefore, in March 1983, the Politburo threw its support behind the Gorbachev proposals to encourage private plot output by such things as allowing collective farms to sell cows or pigs to private farmers who would then raise them. This could be profitable for the collectives because, without requiring great capital outlay, it added a new sideline to their production if they were as ingenious as the one near Penza, which used its resident pensioners to raise piglets that were then sold to the private plot growers. There were some problems with the theory, however, not the least of which was that perennial Russian headache of getting the highly perishable produce of the private plots to market in time and without mishap. But now the scheme, which had been implemented only on a limited scale, was to be tried nationwide.[9]

Andropov at this time was apparently in especially poor health—indeed, he may well have been near death at one stage—and he began to rely increasingly on Gorbachev for various projects. For example, by the spring Gorbachev is believed to have been given additional duties concerned with party personnel outside the purely agricultural sphere. In the closing years of the Brezhnev era, Gorbachev had been in charge of both agriculture-related and other light industry. But in March 1983, the two spheres of authority in the Central Committee bureaucracy were apparently split. However, the light industry section as well as the organizational party work and the administrative organs departments were placed under the supervision of Kapitonov, who had known Gorbachev since his days at Moscow University. At the same time, Gorbachev was designated as the Politburo secretary who supervised Kapitonov.

The implications of this change are significant. It meant that Gorbachev was now moving far beyond the immediate environs of agriculture and into the realm of ideology and cadre selection. It was not lost on many in Moscow and abroad that this was the combination of power bases—agriculture and personnel—that had provided Nikita Khrushchev with his springboard to power in 1953.[10]

And if further proof were needed of Gorbachev's increasing

stature in the Andropov regime, it was certainly provided in May 1983 when he headed a Soviet delegation on a visit to Canada.

Ostensibly, he traveled as head of a Soviet parliamentary delegation—a much-used Soviet pretext for such occasions—but as the visit developed, it was clear that it was designed both as a test of Gorbachev's abilities to deal with Western politicians and, perhaps more important, to show off the bright new figure in the Kremlin. In other words, it would mix examination and exhibition, and for this, in Soviet eyes, Canada was an ideal venue because of its proximity to and similarity to the United States.

During the visit, Gorbachev took the opportunity for meetings with then Prime Minister Trudeau and the leaders of the opposition political parties. But the official highlight of the visit was most unusual. On May 17, 1983, Gorbachev appeared before the standing committee of the House of Commons and the Senate on external affairs and national defense. A ranking member of the Soviet Politburo was subjecting himself to the potentially hostile questions of a largely unknown and unpredictable panel. And the potential for hostility to the Soviet Union among Canadian politicians is real; many of them, themselves, come from the Eastern European communities that make up so much of Canada's population, or they represent constituencies composed of such Ukrainian, Hungarian, Polish, or Russian groups. It was also most certainly on the minds of the Canadian authorities that it was from this section of the Canadian population that had come a physical attack on the last prominent Soviet visitor to Canada, Premier Aleksei Kosygin, in Toronto in 1972. Nor were the committee members unused to such visitors. Earlier in the same session of Parliament, they had subjected President Hosni Mubarak of Egypt, President Mohammed Zia ul-Haq of Pakistan, and Prime Minister Andreas Papandreou of Greece to the same give-and-take treatment.

But Gorbachev took it in his stride, and he obviously had been well briefed. In his opening remarks he dwelt at great length on the dangers of nuclear war and the desirability of a freeze on deployment of nuclear weapons. To Canadians, living in a country that lies geographically between the two nuclear superpowers and over whose territory any hostile missiles would most likely travel in the event of war between them, nuclear disarmament is an especially important topic. So Gorbachev was playing to a receptive audience when he said:

> We in the Soviet Union are sure that the 1970s, which were years of detente, were not an accidental episode in the difficult history of mankind. The policy of detente has not run its course. The term detente has taken a firm place in the political dictionary because the future belongs to detente. We are proceeding on the assumption that Canada is also interested in detente. As far as we are concerned, we will persistently continue to follow a line that will prevent further exacerbation of the international situation and which will not allow the positive potential of detente to be buried. The policy of our government to Canada is consistent and one of principle. We are in favor of good friendly relations with our neighbor across the Pole, of broadening mutually advantageous collaboration in all areas, and the continuation and deepening of political dialogue. Not confrontation but mutually advantageous collaboration—that is our program.[11]

From the beginning, with the question about the Soviet invasion of Afghanistan and direct questions about missile deployment, the Canadians adopted a polite but nevertheless adversary tone in the proceedings. Gorbachev was a little belligerent too. His grip on the nuances and numbers of nuclear policy was surprising. And he was not afraid to speak bluntly. Thus, when one of the questioners asked why it was necessary for the Soviet Union to maintain missile forces in Asia, he replied: "What do you expect from us? There are missiles in South Korea and on ships in the Pacific. The Nakasone Government have agreed to turn Japan into an unsinkable missile carrier, and militaristic plans are being hatched. What position are we to adopt? We cannot ignore the situation." It was obvious that far from being confined to agriculture, this was a man deeply involved in making foreign and defense policy.

Thus, when he was asked a provocative question about Soviet policy toward Poland, he replied with assurance and, moreover, with a hint of a threat. The questioner, a Canadian politician of Polish extraction, had implied that Canada had given a great deal of assistance to the Poles in recent years, in the form of credits to buy grain for example, and wondered why the Moscow regime was not being equally generous. Gorbachev bristled:

We are not indifferent to what is taking place in a fraternal country, and during this period of internal processes and changes in Poland, the western countries have taken the position of an economic blockade of Poland, and have in point of fact compromised the economic relations established with the country. They have deprived the country itself and its enterprises of the opportunity to operate and function normally. This probably got us thinking about the range of cooperation between the socialist and western countries. That is point one; point two is that we, on our part, are helping our Polish friends, the Polish nation. We are helping them in every possible way, financially, economically and in the way of food. The processes in Poland are positive ones.[12]

But Gorbachev also showed just how charming he could be. He praised Prime Minister Trudeau as a statesman who had striven to preserve detente. He even endorsed efforts to resolve that most Canadian of issues, how to reduce the environmental effects of acid rain. He more or less laughed off the question about why the Soviet Union needed so many spies in Canada. And he was unquestionably candid about the defects in the Soviet economy, saying "industrial growth rates have in recent years not suited us." He also admitted that there had been serious problems in food production, and he was careful to thank the Canadian authorities for their cooperative attitude toward selling grain to the Soviet Union. But he also suggested that steps were being taken that he hoped would remedy the farm troubles and with a rueful smile added: "The only thing we really need, so to speak, is a little help from the skies."

One of the Canadian politicians who was particularly involved with the Gorbachev visit was Eugene Whalen, the agriculture minister in the Trudeau government. Whalen had first met Gorbachev during a visit to the Soviet Union in connection with a grain agreement in 1981. At that time, they had talked for an hour or so. But in the spring of 1983 Whalen got a much better opportunity to study the Russian during a tour of almost a week through Canadian farming regions. After the discussions in Ottawa, the journey started with an informal barbecue at the federal agricultural research station in the Canadian capital, where the Canadians noticed that Gorbachev drank very little, limiting himself to a glass or two of wine with his meal. And as they ate three meals together every day and traveled during the next week,

Whalen found Gorbachev to be almost disarmingly frank and a pleasant companion.

From Ottawa, they traveled to Niagara Falls, where they went for the inevitable boat ride on the *Maid of the Mist* underneath the roaring falls. In addition, during a visit to Toronto, they had a meal in the revolving restaurant high up the CN Tower, where Gorbachev surprised Whalen by remarking that the Canadians had upstaged Moscow's own television tower by 20 meters.

Others, too, had noted this attention to detail, and it was to be fully expressed during the remainder of the trip. At the Heinz ketchup factory in Leamington, Ontario, at the giant Hiram Walker distillery in Windsor, Ontario, and at a meat-packing operation in Kitchener, Ontario, Gorbachev meticulously questioned the workers about their pay scales, about their families, about the number of cars they owned, about whether or not they had second, vacation homes, about their children's education, their pensions, and so on. But what he sought to discover most frequently was the incentives that motivated them to work, it seemed to him, so eagerly. Altogether, said Whalen, "he was very inquisitive."

Before leaving for Alberta, the Whalens entertained Gorbachev and the six other members of his party at the Whalen farm on the Detroit River just south of the city of Detroit, in the fertile cash-crop region of Southern Ontario. Then the party flew west to inspect Canadian developments in dry-land and zero-tillage farming, matters of obvious importance to the Soviet Union where climate conditions are comparable. During this extended visit, relations between the two became much more informal—they are both gregarious men—and Whalen thus became the first Western politician to get more than a passing measure of Gorbachev. They talked at length about rural life, and Gorbachev spoke with some vehemence on the need to improve social conditions on the farms of the Soviet Union by building better housing, better schools, and recreation facilities. Whalen also noted that he mentioned with some irritation that Moscow itself was just getting to be too big, and something had to be done about that. Small matters also came up. One of the things that apparently had surprised Gorbachev was the uniform quality of Canadian butter, something that would appeal to someone from a nation where quality control has always been an industrial problem. And Gorbachev talked about his family, especially about his granddaughter, Oksana, who he said was constantly complaining that she never saw him. "You work too hard, Grandpa," he quoted her as saying.[13]

In Calgary he suddenly cut his visit short and flew home two days earlier than originally planned. He had apparently been summoned back to the Soviet Union where important changes in the leadership were already in progress and where, it was to be revealed later, Yuri Andropov was already a dying man.

According to some analysts, at this time there was some renewed resistance to the changes that Andropov proposed for the party and government leadership and, indeed, for Soviet society. In the secretariat, in particular, he was not in a strong position. Therefore, he was forced to seek allies where he could find them. There was already a community of interest between Andropov and Gorbachev about the things that were necessary to improve the economy and particularly the agricultural sphere. But Gorbachev was not the whole Politburo, nor did he control some of the key sections of the secretariat, and Andropov looked outside for further support. An obvious source of backing was in the feisty sixty-year-old Leningrad party secretary, Grigory Romanov. Romanov therefore, in June 1983, was moved to Moscow as a ranking

Central Committee secretary along with Gorbachev and Chernenko. Romanov apparently was placed in overall charge of heavy industry, particularly as it related to defense. This, in addition to helping bolster Andropov's control of the bureaucracy and perhaps of the military, also had the effect of opening up the possibility that Romanov would become Gorbachev's chief eventual rival for the supreme leadership.

Gorbachev and Romanov, however, hardly acted like traditional rivals for the leadership in the Soviet Union. There was nothing about their relationship—at least not that part of it that seems public and still unrehearsed—that overtly involved the deadly atmosphere of similar such rivalries in past Soviet history. Thus, after Romanov's return from a quasi diplomatic mission to Finland in April 1983, when Gorbachev greeted him at Moscow airport the two appeared genuinely pleased to see each other and embraced with beaming smiles. Similarly, when the Supreme Soviet met in June 1983, the two were seated together on the podium, in the row behind the stolid Chernenko and Marshal Ustinov. As television broadcast the speeches of Politburo member Geidar Aliyev and Foreign Minister Andrei Gromyko to the assembly, surprised viewers in Moscow were quick to notice that Gorbachev and Romanov were engaged in spirited and obviously friendly conversation. First one would initiate the dialogue, and then the other would reply. Since little happens by accident in such surroundings, most Soviet citizens took the interchange to mean that when Gorbachev became the supreme leader, he would find a high position in his regime for the congenial Romanov.[14]

It was at this June meeting that Andropov officially became the President of the Soviet Union. The position is largely symbolic, since real power is concentrated in the position of general secretary of the party, but the decision to elevate Andropov to the post relatively early in his regime seemed an indication that he had quickly gained supremacy in the coalition that wielded power. To most eyes, Andropov was undoubtedly the man in charge, able to reward his loyal followers, as in the case of Vitaly Vorotnikov, who was promoted to candidate membership in the Politburo at this time. Later he would become a full voting member, a long way from the semiexile in Cuba he had suffered for offending Leonid Brezhnev. Even though Andropov could offer such rewards, it was also generally agreed that he had been put in power largely through the influence of Marshal Ustinov and Foreign Minister Gromyko, and they seemed to continue to be influential in the way the country was governed.

Chernenko, as the second ranking member of the Politburo and the secretariat, made the nomination. This had two purposes. It added weight to Andropov's designation, but it also added weight to Chernenko's position because such tasks have traditionally been alloted to the party secretary in charge of ideology and personnel. In other words, Chernenko, who had been regarded by many Russian and foreign observers as a has-been, could no longer be so considered. He finally had donned the mantle of the revered Mikhail Suslov.

Chernenko's speech, in which he nominated Andropov for the presidency, was worthy of Suslov in its conservatism. Chernenko inveighed against permissiveness on the part of writers, artists, playwrights and theater directors, and filmmakers. He even criticized a resurgence of religious expression among Soviet citizens. And he attacked the tendency among Russian youth to adopt Western habits. It was time, he urged, that the intensity of party indoctrination be increased and that "positive heroes" be cultivated.

One key aspect of the Suslov domain, dealing with foreign Communists, seems to have been denied him. That role was reserved for Andropov himself as long as he was capable although, to judge by his gaunt and stooped appearance at the plenum, he would not be capable much longer. Nevertheless, Andropov was still able to carry a strong message to the party faithful, exhorting them to do more than merely pay lip service to seeking progress. "What good can a meeting do," he asked, "if, as so often happens, it is held according to a prepared script, if there is no interested, frank discussion, if statements are edited beforehand while initiative and especially criticism are smoothed over and muffled?"

But Andropov seemed to be shouting into the wind, and the meeting did not really come to grips with the economic difficulties that bedeviled the nation. The very intransigence of the bureaucracy cast an almost pathetic pallor over the proceedings as the obviously frail Andropov urged them to greater activity. It seemed, however, that few were listening to his message: "It is one thing to proclaim socialism as one's goal and quite another to build it."

It was a gallant effort from a man who obviously knew his own severe physical limitations. It was almost as if he realized that the session was a last chance to get things moving. From that time on, he was seen less and less, and as the year wore on, Mikhail Gorbachev frequently deputized for him.[15]

Indeed, during the spring and early summer of 1983, Gorbachev was achieving unusual prominence in the regime. In addition to the new responsibilities he had gained in light industry, he apparently at this time became the Central Committee secretary charged with supervision of party personnel. This was an especially key opportunity, since party elections were soon to be held, starting in November 1983, and the man who controlled the personnel department was in an excellent position to place his own supporters in strategic places for any future leadership election.[16]

And more and more, Gorbachev was emerging as a figure to be reckoned with in the ideological leadership of the party. In April, for example, he was chosen to speak on behalf of the leadership at ceremonies marking the annual commemoration of Lenin's birth. Andropov had delivered the Lenin memorial address the year previously. This was Gorbachev's first speech of an ideological nature to be given such publicity, including front-page display in *Pravda*. In it, Gorbachev stayed close to the usual phraseology that places Lenin at least on a par with Marx in the Communist pantheon. But in addition, he took the opportunity to link their teachings to the campaign originated by Andropov to improve production in the Soviet Union. "In these decisions," he said, "the Soviet people see a consistent continuation of the Leninist course of the party, its internal and external policies. The workers fully approve and support the measures carried out by the Politburo for improving the work of the state and economic organs, the strengthening of discipline and order, the raising of responsibility of the cadres, the strict observance of laws, for the further growth of the economic potential of the country, for the reliable guaranteeing of the interests of the security of the Soviet Union, our allies and friends...."[17]

During this period important developments were taking place in the way Soviet industry and, once again, agriculture were organized. In April 1983, a draft law had been published dealing with work collectives for industrial projects. These collectives consisted of the workers involved in the project who were to be permitted to organize and hold meetings—in fact it was to be required that no fewer than two meetings a year would be held—at which they would propose changes in the way their enterprise was being conducted. The management was "required" to consider their proposals although the managers would retain the last word on what was finally done. Particular emphasis was to be paid to discipline in the work place. In addition, the workers were also urged to create work brigades. In this arrangement, those employed in a specific area of an enterprise or in a separate enterprise could band together, under the supervision of a party-appointed leader, to decide how to organize the project and how to divide the payment. To outside observers it looked much like the introduction of a profit motive.

The Yugoslavs had introduced similar ideas many years previously, and the Hungarians also had moved to reorganize their agriculture and industry along similar lines. Andropov, because of his long service in Hungary, was receptive to the Hungarian model, and Gorbachev apparently had become so too. Over the years he had become familiar with the Hungarian party leadership and did so again at extensive talks that were held in the Kremlin at the end of July 1983. Gorbachev, in fact, seems to have been the prime host for the Hungarian visitors on this occasion, conducting Kadar and his aides on a visit to the Moscow Auto Works. But during that month, Andropov also seems to have regained some of his vigor and was able to meet not only the Hungarian delegation but also Chancellor Helmut Kohl of West Germany and his foreign minister, Hans-Dietrich Genscher, plus visiting French and Portuguese Communist Party delegations. And, in another sign that he was again able to concentrate on his campaign against inefficiency, *Pravda* began to criticize the perennial problems with the nation's transportation system.[18]

However, by the late months of the year, as Andropov's health apparently began to decline seriously, again Gorbachev, more and more, was being delegated to deal with foreign Communist parties, both those who governed their countries and those not in power, as well as foreign delegations from non-Communist countries. In this vein, it was natural that in August he would greet a parliamentary delegation from Canada when it visited Moscow. Similarly, on October 18, he paid a visit to Hungary for talks with Janos Kadar and other leaders. And, late in December 1983, he made another foreign diplomatic journey, this time to Portugal, where the veteran Communist leader, Alvaro Cunhal, was facing re-election as the leader of the party. Gorbachev's presence at the meeting in Oporto had significance outside Portugal. At the same time that the Portuguese Communists were dutifully returning their seventy-year-old pro-Moscow chieftan to office, in neighboring Spain the Communist Party was re-electing as its leader, Gerardo Iglesias, an adherent of the Eurocommunist philosophy that emphasizes political and ideological independence from the Kremlin. Gorbachev's speech was therefore directed not only to the Oporto audience but to the Spanish Communists. In addition, he raised the same issues he had in Canada, which the whole Soviet hierarchy had been emphasizing.

> The things that worry you, the Portuguese Communists, today—the growing tension in the world and the real threat of nuclear war—also worry our people and our party. The situation in the world has become really alarming. It calls for vigilance, it demands activity on the part of all those who are sincerely interested in guaranteeing a peaceful future for the present and future generations. . . .
>
> The essence of the present militaristic course of the U.S.A. is to ensure for itself a dominating position in the world, without considering the rights and interests of other states and peoples. For this reason the military potential of the U.S.A. is being strengthened, and the large-scale programs of production of newer and newer types of weapons, the militarization of the oceans and of outer space, are being real-

ized. For this reason the military presence of the U.S.A. is being expanded many thousands of kilometers away from American territory; the interventionist "rapid deployment forces" have been formed; bridgeheads for armed intervention in the affairs of other states are being created—be it in Central America or in the Near East, in the zone of the Pacific or the Indian Oceans, or in other regions of the world. . . .

In the U.S.A. it is argued at an official level that normal relations with the U.S.S.R. can only be carried out when the U.S.S.R. has changed its social system. The openly stated objective in Washington is the achievement of military superiority over the U.S.S.R., over world socialism.[19]

Apart from the hostile tone it exhibited toward the United States, the speech was notable for several other things. Gorbachev took great care to pay repeated tribute to Yuri Andropov, recalling Andropov speeches and statements to bolster his own argument. And the statement also was notable for its frankness on the high cost of its military apparatus to the Soviet Union. "This attainment of equilibrium [in military capability] demanded a great deal of effort from the Soviet people," he said. Then he went on to suggest that further economic effort would be required.

We attach the highest priority to areas of economic and political work such as raising the effectiveness of production through its intensification, materially enhancing labor productivity based on faster scientific and technical progress, solving the problems of food and energy, further improving the mechanisms of socialist management with a view to expanding the initiative of enterprises and individual collectives and giving them a greater voice in the process of planning and the implementation of plans; and, in the last analysis, increasing the efficiency of the entire economy.[20]

It was a forceful statement, worthy of Andropov himself, but yet also in tune with what seemed to be the current thinking of such people as Gromyko and Marshal Ustinov. It was a very public presentation of a forceful new personality in the Kremlin.

There was much less publicity, however, for Gorbachev and the other non-military leaders of the Soviet Union in another major incident. That was in the tragic episode of the South Korean airliner shot down over the Sea of Japan on September 1, 1983, while flying from New York to Seoul, by way of Anchorage, Alaska. At first the Soviet authorities did not acknowledge that the plane had been shot down. Only when they could no longer evade the issue did they admit that the South Korean plane, with 269 people on board, had been downed by a missile fired from a Soviet interceptor aircraft. The Soviet statement insisted that the Korean plane had strayed over Soviet territory, including highly sensitive military bases on the island of Sakhalin and the Kamchatka Peninsula. Like all the other members of the Politburo, Gorbachev was largely on the sidelines in responding to the outcry over the incident. It was initially left to Marshal Nikolai Ogarkov, at a highly unusual Moscow press conference, to try to explain away what had obviously been a colossal political blunder by suggesting that the plane had been on a spy mission for the Central Intelligence Agency.

To some observers, it seemed that there had been a failure of leadership in the sequence of events that had led to the shooting down of the Korean plane, perhaps even such a monumental failure that the military had acted on its own without recourse to the civilian party leadership. Further, it seems highly likely that there was some friction between the military establishment and the party hierarchy at this time, possibly involving the strong personalities of Nikolai Ogarkov and Mikhail Gorbachev directly. In the event, Ogarkov eventually was to apparently overstep himself and be removed from the center of power. But the doubts about the leadership that first seemed to arise at the time of the Korean airliner incident, by the time the Central Committee held a two-day meeting at the end of the year, had crystalized to such an extent that it was only too apparent that, such a short time after Brezhnev's death, another power vacuum had again enveloped the Soviet Union. Andropov sent a message to the plenum: "I deeply regret that because of temporary causes, I will not be able to attend the sessions."

For the first time, the Soviet authorities were admitting that a Soviet leader was to miss such an important occasion. Although proclamations continued to be made in his name, Andropov himself had not been seen in public for more than three months. On November 7, Soviet citizens were given ample evidence of the seriousness of his condition when he was absent from the Lenin Mausoleum balcony during the parade marking the 1917 Bolshevik Revolution. Then, ten days later, Andropov was too weak to take part in one of those carefully staged Soviet propaganda events. The occasion was a meeting with John Crystal, a banker from Coon Rapids, Iowa, who was visiting Moscow. Some weeks earlier, the editor of the *Des Moines Register* had written an open letter to Andropov recalling that in 1959 Nikita Khrushchev had visited the fertile farms of Iowa and that the visit had raised hopes for peace in the world. He invited Andropov to make a similar visit with a similar purpose in mind. However, Andropov couldn't even meet the Iowa banker in the Kremlin, and Gorbachev had to deputize for him in delivering a reply.

The message that Gorbachev relayed was that Andropov shared with the people of Iowa "the sentiments of anxiety over the situation in the world, the state of relations between the United States and the USSR." Whether or not the words were those of Andropov or Gorbachev, they were to be quite similar to views expressed more frequently when Gorbachev's power had obviously grown in the Soviet Union.

The signs were unmistakable that the general secretary was in poor condition physically, but there were also signs that Andropov was still vigorously pursuing the renovation of the leadership that he had sought from the start of his term in office. Men who were recognized as his supporters were being steadily promoted in the bureaucracy. And at the December Central Committee meeting, fifty-seven-year-old Vitaly Vorotnikov, the Premier of the Russian Republic and the man who had been demoted to the Cuban embassy as he felt Brezhnev's vengeance in the wake of the Medunov affair, was promoted from candidate member to full voting member of the Politburo.

Andropov had brought him back from Cuba and charged him with cleansing the corruption in the Krasnodar region. That done, in June Vorotnikov had been named Premier of the Russian Republic, the Soviet Union's largest constituent part, and an alternate member of the Politburo. Now, six months later, he had taken a further, major step upward. The general belief was that he was a likely successor to Soviet Premier Nikolai Tikhonov.

In addition, another Andropov associate, Viktor Chebrikov, the sixty-year-old head of the KGB, was named a candidate member of the Politburo, and Yegor Ligachev, a former Suslov protégé, was named the Central Committee secretary responsible for cadres. A fourth appointment, of Mikhail

Solomentsev as a full Politburo member, was seen as a set-back for the Brezhnev faction of the leadership that was now grouped behind Chernenko. Solomentsev had been a candidate member of the Politburo for a dozen years, his promotion reportedly blocked by Brezhnev because Solomentsev had supported Frol Kozlov, his one-time rival for the leadership.

It was clear that Andropov was seeking to revitalize the leadership by injecting new bodies into the upper echelons. And from a speech that was read for him at the Central Committee meeting, it was also clear that even though he was disabled he was in no mood to abandon the campaigns he had launched for greater efficiency and productivity and for the elimination of corruption and malingering. He said that the program had the full support of the party. "A great deal has been achieved, but much is still to be done," he said. "This places great responsibility on all of us, on everyone without exception, and we should justify this profound confidence of the people."

In many ways the words were those same cliches that had echoed from the rostrums of the Brezhnev era, and in many ways his long service as head of the KGB had rendered Andropov a suspicious figure to the Soviet people, but there was no mistaking that most common people had welcomed his attempts to stir the country from the lethargic monotony in which it had droned on for so long.

His absence from the December meetings, however, meant that it had been well over four months since he had appeared in public, the last time being on August 18, when he had met with a group of United States senators. Now, he had missed the November ceremonies in Red Square and the Central Committee sessions in the Kremlin, unheard of in previous Soviet history.[21] Most Soviet citizens expected any day to hear the solemn music and to see the rest of the rites that mark the passage of a leadership in Moscow, but Andropov himself seemed, even at this time, to be determined to push ahead younger men who would carry on the plans.

By early February 1984, it was reported that at least nineteen of the one hundred and fifty or so regional first secretaries had been replaced in a round of elections supervised by Gorbachev. In addition, fifteen other secretaries of similar rank had been replaced earlier during the Andropov regime. Knowledgeable observers said that there had not been such a housecleaning in the upper echelons of the party since the early years of Leonid Brezhnev when he was trying to cement his grip on power in the face of opposition from Podgorny and Shelepin. And if these new men moving up in the hierarchy were Andropov's followers, it is also probably true that they were Gorbachev's people as well. Because, it was generally believed—by Russians as well as foreigners—that Andropov was largely functioning at this time through Gorbachev, who was said to be a frequent visitor to the clinic where the general secretary was said to be hospitalized.[22]

In addition, other Gorbachev supporters were being installed in key positions throughout the country. For example, when Vorotnikov became the Premier of the Russian Republic, his place in Krasnodar was taken by forty-seven-year-old Georgii Razumovsky. Like Gorbachev, Razumovsky had a background in the Komsomol, but more significantly, in the 1960s and 1970s he had been engaged in party work in Krasnodar while Gorbachev had been rising up the party ladder in neighboring Stavropol and had recently been working directly under Gorbachev in the agricultural bureaucracy in Moscow.

The signs of Gorbachev's new status were also becoming increasingly obvious. When, in Leningrad, a new party secretary was elected in July 1983 to replace Romanov, after he had been moved to Moscow, Gorbachev was chosen for the task of nominating him. And astute Soviet citizens were quick to notice the treatment accorded him on the visit. He was taken for public visits to the Lenin Museum and to the old cruiser *Aurora*, real chief-of-state-treatment, as one analyst described it.[23]

But for some of the Soviet leadership, perhaps, it was too early for such regal treatment. Although among the thirteen members of the Politburo, Andropov could count on a majority to support him, there was certainly no guarantee at this time that they would support Gorbachev. Indeed, the forces of conservatism in the persons of Chernenko, Tikhonov, Foreign Minister Gromyko, and, perhaps most importantly, Defense Minister Ustinov, really constituted the largest bloc in the leadership. Gromyko and Ustinov were especially important because they represented what might be called neutral blocs within the leadership. Both were of such an age and inclination that their ambitions for the ultimate leadership had long ago been put to rest, and their votes in any leadership contest would be expected to favor the status quo. That did not augur well for Gorbachev's chances.

Throughout the early part of the winter, the uncertainty continued. As usual, the Soviet public and the rest of the world were told nothing of what ailment Andropov suffered from except for unofficial murmurings about a cold. But gradually the word began to seep out that the Soviet leader was suffering from a seriously debilitating kidney disease. For the Soviet people, who had been so quick to place new hope for a better life in Andropov's campaigns against corruption and inefficiency, the disappointment was widespread and real.

Then, in the early afternoon of February 10, 1983, radio and television stations in Moscow began playing the telltale

solemn music that has always been followed by solemn pro-
nouncements. Then, at 2:30 P.M., the announcer revealed that
at 4:50 on the previous afternoon, Yuri Andropov's heart and
kidneys had finally given out. The official death announcement seemed to emphasize the collective nature of the leadership that would follow him. It promised that the party would
continue Andropov's domestic campaigns to improve industrial efficiency and to seek peaceful coexistence with the
United States and other western nations. "The Soviet people
are convinced opponents of the settlement of contentious
international issues by force," the statement said. "A world
without wars is our ideal. We want to live in peace with all
countries and to cooperate actively with the governments and
organizations that are prepared to work honestly and con-
structively in the name of peace."[24]

After less than fifteen months, the Soviet leadership was
thrown into the turmoil surrounding the choice of a new
leader. For the Moscow leadership it was obviously a time of
crisis. There were serious lessons to be learned from the
events surrounding the choice of Yuri Andropov, but would
they profit by them? For example, the official medical bul-
letin on Andropov's death revealed what had been widely
suspected, that the dead leader had been in failing health
almost from the moment he took office and in fact had suffered total kidney failure in February 1983. Would the Soviet
leaders therefore turn to one of the younger and more vigor-
ous personalities like Romanov or Gorbachev or would they
choose an older, interim leader, perhaps even one like Chernenko, who reportedly suffered severely from emphysema, or
Marshal Ustinov, who had frequently been reported in poor
health?[25]

Once again, after such a brief interlude, the Soviet Union
was to witness the full solemnity of the funeral of a general

secretary and President. Andropov's bier was laid out on the second floor of the House of Unions, surrounded by the medals and awards he had been given over the years. An orchestra played solemn music by Chopin, Beethoven, and Tchaikovsky as the mourners, bused in for the occasion from the city and suburbs, trooped past. In line with previous custom, the full Politburo came together to pay their last respects. Chernenko was most prominently placed at the center of the line, with Tikhonov and Gromyko on his right side. At his left was Gorbachev, with Romanov beside him. It was as if the generational division had been solemnized. After a brief vigil, the Politburo members moved around the casket to console Andropov's wife and family. When Andropov's son, Igor, a member of the diplomatic corps, was greeted by Marshal Ustinov, he lowered his head and wept. Foreign Minister Gromyko and Gorbachev hastened to comfort and reassure him while the rest of the Politburo marched out. It was a sadly human moment amid so much funereal pomp.[26]

Finally, on February 14 before representatives of 111 countries, Andropov's funeral was held in Red Square. Chernenko, Marshal Ustinov and Gromyko delivered the eulogies. Then Andropov was lowered into his last resting place between Dzerzhinsky, the first chief of what was to become the KGB and over which Andropov had ruled for so long, and Mikhail Kalinin, the nominal head of state for twenty-seven years, starting in 1919. As the casket was borne to the grave, Chernenko was the leading honorary pallbearer, at the left front of the coffin. Directly opposite him, on the right side, was Mikhail Gorbachev. The arrangement seemed significant to Russians and Westerners alike.

5

The
Interval
Under
Chernenko

IT WAS apparent from the announcement of the arrangements for Yuri Andropov's funeral that the Soviet leadership had placed the value of the status quo above the need
for revitalization of the upper reaches of the party and the
government.

Konstantin Chernenko's role as chairman of the funeral
commission for Andropov and his role in leading the eulogies
immediately told the Russian people that he was to be the new
General Secretary of the party. But there were also signs that
the younger members of the leadership were slowly gaining
influence, even if power was not yet within their grasp. Gorbachev's prominent role in the funeral seemed to indicate
that. And further proof was given at the Central Committee
plenum called to elect the new leader.

As expected, Chernenko was nominated by Tikhonov to
succeed Andropov as the new General Secretary and was duly
elected by the three hundred committee members. But at the
close of the meeting, it was Gorbachev who endorsed the

choice of Chernenko and called for unity in the party and the regime to carry out the program initiated by Andropov. Gorbachev's speech followed the precedent set by Chernenko when Andropov had been elected leader; now the Gorbachev speech seemed to indicate that he had been confirmed as the heir apparent to Chernenko. However, there was an apparently important difference between Chernenko's nomination of Andropov and Gorbachev's speech on this occasion. Chernenko in 1982 had spoken "on the instructions of the Politburo." Gorbachev spoke "in the name of the Politburo." The difference was important. Chernenko had spoken as a messenger. Gorbachev, his listeners quickly understood, spoke with the full authority of a Suslov, a person of great importance in the leadership.[1]

But there were also some puzzling features about the Gorbachev speech. The fact that he had made such a statement was not publicly revealed immediately, possibly indicating that there had been some friction among the leadership or that the balance that had been struck was uneasy.

It was a notable comeback for Chernenko. In the first months after Andropov had come to power, it seemed to Russians and foreign analysts alike, that time had passed Chernenko by, that Brezhnev's apparent desire to see his long-time associate follow him in office would not be fulfilled. Moreover, there were frequent reports that he had been ill, perhaps even seriously so and his appearance, white-haired, stooped, and showing difficulty in walking, seemed to indicate that was the case. Now, there he was, general secretary of the party and acting like it.

Chernenko had been born in the Krasnoyarsk region of Siberia on September 24, 1911, making him seventy-two years old when he finally reached the general secretaryship. Despite his Ukrainian-sounding surname he was of Russian origin, a crucial requirement. He had joined the party in 1931, the year of Gorbachev's birth. His party and service record were modest. His only military service, for example, had been as a youthful border guard in the early 1930s; supposedly that had caused some of the Red Army figures to treat him with some disdain. His rise to the central organs of the party came with his association with Leonid Brezhnev in Moldavia, the small section of the southwestern Soviet Union that is set apart as a separate constituent republic. After the fall of Khrushchev and the installation of Brezhnev he became a Central Committee secretary in 1976, a candidate member of the Politburo in 1977, and a full, voting, member a year later. Although he had been showered with many awards, including the Lenin Prize at home, and presentations from several of the Soviet Union's allies, his chief virtue seemed to be to serve as a sort of chief aide for Brezhnev. It had not been a greatly distinguished career. There had been no great projects like the Moscow subway in his record. He had never run a huge operation like the KGB. He had traveled fairly extensively, including a visit to America in 1974, and in his first speech to the Central Committee he endorsed Andropov's domestic policies and offered a loaded olive branch to the United States.

"We need no military superiority," he said. "We do not intend to dictate our will to others. But we will not permit the military equilibrium that has been achieved to be upset. And let nobody have even the slightest doubt about that. We will further see to it that our country's defense capacity be strengthened, that we should have enough means to cool the hot heads of militant adventurists."[2]

But, if Chernenko had been promoted, Gorbachev had also moved up a notch in the hierarchy, and evidence of that was provided a few days later. Protocol is strict in the Soviet

Union. That had been shown in the funeral rites for Andropov. It had been shown again in the Central Committee plenum that had chosen Chernenko. And now it was being displayed in the campaign—if campaign is the right word—for elections to the Supreme Soviet, the nation's nominal parliament.

The usual practice in such elections is that the various members of the leadership make their campaign speeches in strict order of precedence, the nearer the election date the speech is made, the higher the speaker's position in the hierarchy. In February 1984, Chernenko, as party leader, spoke last, Tikhonov, as government leader, second last. Gorbachev spoke third last, after such figures as Foreign Minister Gromyko, Defense Minister Ustinov, and other members of the Politburo. The content of his speech, given in the North Caucasus village of Ipatovo, not far from Stavropol, was also significant. Gorbachev made it clear that he stood for the same things that had been important to Andropov. The priorities that he listed for the Soviet Union were those that Andropov had set out when he had come to power just eighteen months earlier: modernizing industrial technology; tightening labor discipline; combating corruption; improving management in industry; and, especially important to Gorbachev, increasing agricultural production. It was a stern speech, as Gorbachev spoke of a need for "further enforcing order, being more exacting, organized, and disciplined, and waging an uncompromising struggle with the negative phenomena that come into conflict with our morals and with socialist legality." In addition, Gorbachev echoed recent cool remarks by Marshal Ustinov and Foreign Minister Gromyko toward the United States, especially as far as nuclear arms negotiations were concerned.[3]

Further confirmation of Gorbachev's status was given in a March 15 interview that Viktor Afanasyev, the chief editor of *Pravda*, gave to the Swedish newspaper *Dagens Nyheter*. Afanasyev, over the years, has gained a reputation as being uncommonly frank in discussions with foreigners. On this occasion, instead of avoiding the question as other Russian officials might have done, he promptly said that he thought Mikhail Gorbachev would succeed Chernenko as the next Russian leader. The *Pravda* editor also told his Swedish interviewer that Gorbachev had now been given the task of supervising the work of the Central Committee Secretariat, previously the domain of Mikhail Suslov. However, Afanasyev also made clear that this did not mean that Gorbachev had taken over the ideological watchdog role that Suslov had also held; that, he said, had been reserved for himself by Chernenko.[4]

Then, on April 11, 1984, at the first session of the new Supreme Soviet it was Gorbachev who rose to nominate Chernenko for the Presidency of the Soviet Union. His speech at that time was especially noteworthy, for it enunciated clearly what had been a developing trend, that whoever held the position of general secretary of the party, should also hold the presidency. Said Gorbachev:

> Relying on the experience of party and state construction in recent years and proceeding from the lofty interests of Soviet society and state, the plenum of the Central Committee has deemed it essential that the general secretary of our party, Konstantin Ustinovich Chernenko, should simultaneously hold the post of chairman of the Presidium of the Supreme Soviet of the U.S.S.R. . . . . At the same time, the execution by the general secretary of the C.P.S.U. Central Committee of

the functions of the chairman of the Presidium of the Supreme Soviet of the U.S.S.R. is of enormous importance for the conduct of the foreign policy of the Soviet Union.[5]

Gorbachev made all the right gestures. He described Chernenko as a "tested leader of the Leninist type." He even went so far as to say that Chernenko's speeches "contain an extensive constructive program for the socio-economic and political development of our country and for improving the international situation." That, said the official Soviet newspapers, drew stormy, prolonged applause, the catch phrase used only for the most important leaders.[6]

But Chernenko was also capable of making a gesture in Gorbachev's direction. In his brief acceptance speech, he touched on Gorbachev's pet theme of increasing productivity to improve the general standard of living. He said: "Today, as never before, carefully considered decisions and outstanding organization are needed to substantially raise the cost-effectiveness of the economy and, on that basis, to improve invariably the well-being of all Soviet people."

At the same session, Gorbachev himself was elected chairman of the foreign affairs commission of the Council of the Union, the more prestigious of the two chambers of the Soviet Parliament. This was an important step in a new direction for the man who up until this time had been best known for his work in agriculture and the economy. Suslov had held the position for two decades, and after his death it had been held by Chernenko. In his nomination speech for Chernenko, Gorbachev had himself outlined the key role of the position. "K. U. Chernenko headed the Foreign Affairs Commission of the Council of the Union of the U.S.S.R. Supreme Soviet," said Gorbachev, "which under his leadership actively implemented the foreign policy course of our party and state."[7]

This new foreign policy position, especially as it involved foreign Communist parties, was the reason Gorbachev was chosen to represent the Soviet Union at the funeral in Rome for Enrico Berlinguer, the Italian Communist leader, in the middle of June 1984. Over the years, the Italian Communist Party had provided plenty of problems for the rulers in Moscow. Berlinguer had been a particular source of irritation over the years, with his espousal of the so-called historical compromise, the behind-the-scenes alliance with the Roman Catholic church and the Christian Democratic Party, and his share in the development of an independent-minded Euro-communism. There was a Moscow-line section of the Italian party, but it was in a decided minority. Most of the Italian Communists were much closer to the pragmatic ideology of the Spanish party and the progressive wing of the French party than they were to the conservative leadership in the Kremlin.[8] Now Gorbachev was apparently being sent to judge the situation in Italy and to meet representatives from most other Communist parties represented at the ceremony.

During the summer, Gorbachev continued to stand out among the Politburo as age and illness gradually began to take their toll of his colleagues. At the Friendship Games, organized by the Soviet Union, after Moscow had decided on a boycott of the Olympic Games in Los Angeles, he was in the most prominent position as he accompanied Marshal Ustinov and other Politburo members to the opening ceremonies. For an hour and a half Gorbachev and the other dignitaries sat in their special box while the athletes paraded. The ceremony was capped with a specially composed song: "To a sunny peace, yes, yes. To a nuclear blast, no, no, no."

In more consequential affairs, too, more and more it was Gorbachev who seemed to be in charge. While Grigory

Romanov was delegated to make a ceremonial visit to Finland, which he had visited many times previously while he was Leningrad party chief, it was Gorbachev who hastened to Sofia on an urgent mission in late summer. The matter at issue was the relationship between the Eastern Bloc and West Germany. During the ceremonial surrounding Andropov's funeral, Chancellor Helmut Kohl and the East German leader Erich Honecker had held discussions in Moscow about improving relations between the two Germanys. In Moscow again in June, Honecker had reportedly cleared with Chernenko his plan to visit West Germany, the first such journey by an East German leader. And there were other tangible signs that relations between the two Germanys were improving. For example, in the summer Bonn publicly announced provision of a $330 million line of bank credit to the Honecker regime. That promptly set off attacks in Moscow, which apparently saw the growing friendship as undermining the Kremlin's campaign to keep new United States missiles out of Western Europe as well as a dangerous exhibition of independence in East Berlin.

The apparent rapprochement between the Germanys was but one sign of a realignment in Europe, particularly in the east. In addition to his projected visit to Bonn, Honecker, normally the most conservative of the satellite leaders, planned a journey to Bucharest for consultations with Nicolae Ceausescu, the Romanian chieftan with whom he and the other Warsaw Pact nations had frequently been at odds. In addition, Ceausescu himself had scheduled a trip to West Germany, and the Bulgarian party chief, Todor Zhivkov, announced he was planning the same journey as well.

It was a most unusual burst of East-West diplomacy, especially since it was widely reported, and apparently believed in East Berlin and elsewhere to have been personally approved by the general secretary of the Communist Party of the Soviet Union. However, during the summer Chernenko disappeared from public view. Simultaneously, the Soviet press launched a strident campaign attacking what seemed to be the accommodation between Bonn and East Berlin. Finally, on September 4, Honecker announced the postponement of his trip to the west. Against that background, the other Eastern European allies of the Soviet Union also appeared to get caught up in the crosscurrents of conflicting signals emanating from Moscow. In Sofia on September 4, even as Honecker was cancelling his trip, a Bulgarian official was still telling an American journalist that Zhivkov would travel to Bonn later that month, as planned.

Four days later, Mikhail Gorbachev arrived in Sofia. That night, Bulgaria's ambassador in Bonn told the West German government that the trip had been canceled. The official reason was to protest deployment of new missiles in Europe by the United States and "hostile" maneuvers by the North Atlantic Treaty Organization. During Gorbachev's visit to Sofia, a rally was staged to mark the fortieth anniversary of the establishment of Communist rule in Bulgaria. With Gorbachev sitting nearby, Zhivkov told the paraders: "Through rapidly accelerating the arms race, the imperialists and above all the U.S. imperialists strive at achieving military, strategic, and political superiority over the countries of real socialism and are preparing themselves for a third world war."[9]

If ever there had been a clash of generations, it was personified in the meeting of the seventy-three-year-old Zhivkov and Gorbachev. While working as an apprentice printer, Zhivkov had been involved in the underground Bulgarian Komsomol movement as far back as 1930, before Gorbachev was born. For his membership in the party, Zhivkov had been arrested and tortured by the pre-World War II Bulgarian government. During the war he had fought against the Germans as a partisan and in the fall of 1944 he is said to have led the detachments that liberated Sofia, the capital. After a brief coalition interregnum, the Communists under Georgi Dimitrov took complete power, but it was not until 1954, after the death of Dimitrov and after a Khrushchev-like upheaval in the Bulgarian party, that Zhivkov became the head of the party. From then on, under both Khrushchev and Brezhnev he had been Moscow's most loyal client, ready with Pavlovian responses to whatever campaign the Kremlin wanted to undertake. Now he was apparently responding to the wrong bell, and it was Gorbachev's task to get him back in line. Whatever argument Gorbachev used, it certainly worked quickly.

It was left to Nicolae Ceausescu to again pursue his independent policies. During the Los Angeles Olympics, the Rumanian team had been the lone Russian-aligned Communist nation to send a team of athletes to compete. Now, in the middle of October Ceausescu went ahead with his visit to West Germany. He did soften the blow to the Warsaw Pact unity by speaking out strongly against the United States missile deployment, but he also emphasized that it was for Europeans, as much as the two superpowers, to decide their own nuclear policies.

Ceausescu was not quite alone in making an overture to the West. At the same time, Janos Kadar, the Hungarian leader, paid a brief visit to France. But France's role in NATO is not seen to be as crucial as West Germany's, and therefore the Kadar trip was less of an irritation to Moscow. But it did give Western reporters a chance to question a high Communist official about the seeming inconsistencies exhibited by the Moscow leadership. Kadar refused to be drawn into any guessing games. "It is a stable leadership," he said, "and the continuity of its leadership is the mark of its stability."[10]

The general belief in the West was that the episode had revealed serious policy differences in the Kremlin, with the ultimate decision on foreign policy having been made by Foreign Minister Gromyko, with the probable backing of Marshal Ustinov, and not by President Chernenko, who had given the impression that he favored the exchanges. That apparent weakness heightened a belief already current in Eastern Europe that Chernenko, for whatever reason he had been chosen to succeed Andropov, was really of no great consequence. Many Eastern Europeans therefore regarded the Chernenko regime as merely a transition. For example, one official in Budapest told James M. Markham of *The New York Times* at this juncture: "This is not a reform period in the Soviet Union. This is a pre-reform period."[11]

In other words, the satellites were looking forward to the time when, they fully expected, Mikhail Gorbachev would become the real leader in Moscow. And Gorbachev's role in the Honecker and Zhivkov affair, too, was enlightening. For the first time he was cast in the role of the heavy, bringing about the abrupt change of plans in Sofia. In addition, he was seen as being aligned with Gromyko, a new connection but an important one in the intricate pattern of Gorbachev's political alliances.

Chernenko's condition about this time began to be the source of another spate of rumors in Moscow and abroad. After July 15, when he left the Soviet capital for his vacation in the Crimea, he was not seen in public for several weeks. And, contrary to the usual Soviet custom—even under Andropov—the Soviet press did not contain articles about his meetings with foreign and domestic dignitaries to give the impression that the general secretary was working, even while on holiday. At this time the Czechoslovakian President, Gustav Husak, was reported to have been in the same area without having met Chernenko. Was the pattern of Brezhnev and Andropov being repeated all over again, and so soon?

Gorbachev, by contrast, was apparently busy in the capital. And once again, it was Viktor Afanasyev, the editor of *Pravda*, who provided some inkling of Gorbachev's enlarged responsibilities. In answering questions about the health of President Chernenko, Afanasyev referred to Gorbachev as a "second general secretary." There is no such official title in the Soviet hierarchy, but the implication in Afanasyev's remarks was that Gorbachev had taken over at least some of the functions normally carried out by the head of the party, in this case Chernenko. The *Pravda* editor's description matched the observations of Western journalists and diplomats; they noted that on the few occasions that Chernenko had appeared in public, Gorbachev had stood at the leader's right hand, normally the spot reserved in Soviet protocol for the second ranking personality. Previously, it had usually been occupied by Marshal Ustinov, Premier Tikhonov, or even Foreign Minister Gromyko.[12]

But Gorbachev's eminence was not so publicly clear when, late in October, the Central Committee met. The plenum devoted most of its sessions to the vexing problems of agriculture. In recent years, Gorbachev would have been most prominent in these discussions; late in 1984 he suddenly took no public part. The biggest decision taken by the committee was to pass a resolution calling for a marked and swift increase in land reclamation, a program which Chernenko called "the decisive factor for further developing agriculture and steadily expanding the country's food stock." Chernenko said, according to the Tass account of the sessions, that "in a com-

paratively short time it is planned to extend the area of irri-
gated and drained lands by 50 percent, which will make it
possible to double the crop output there. As a result, the
country will be able to produce nearly one-half of its gross
crop harvest irrespective of weather fluctuations."[13]

Although Gorbachev was not listed as a major participant
in the discussions, the emphasis on irrigation and reclaiming
marginal land in places where weather would not be a factor
sounded as if it would be attractive to someone who, as a
youth, had spent some chilly days fighting the weather on a
cabless combine near Stavropol.

Whether or not Gorbachev had a hand in forming the
revised agricultural policy, a few weeks later two prominent
businessmen from the United States emerged from a meeting
with Gorbachev convinced that he was the man in charge. The
two Americans were Dwayne O. Andreas, chairman of the
Archer-Daniels-Midland food processing company of De-
catur, Illinois, and James H. Giffen, the former vice-president
of Armco, the steel company. They were in Moscow as representatives of the US-USSR Trade and Economic Council, of
which Andreas is chairman and Giffen the president. The
group was set up by the American and Soviet governments in
1973 to facilitate trade between the two countries.

The meeting took place in Gorbachev's office in the Central
Committee Building and lasted about two hours. Andreas
was impressed by the Russian, finding him "amiable, with an
open personality, frank—seemingly frank—and inquiring."
The American said he sensed that Gorbachev's priority was
working over the Soviet Union's agriculture problems and
that he exhibited a "remarkable knowledge" of a whole range
of related subjects. The frankness was exhibited when the
question of United States trade embargoes was raised.

According to Andreas, Gorbachev was quite concerned as to whether, if new trade agreements were made with the United States, "the sanctity of the contract" would be maintained. And Gorbachev was frank enough to point out that because of the previous grain embargo, the Soviet Union had rearranged its trade, particularly in grain imports, so that it was more reliant on such countries as Canada, Argentina, and France, which he said had proven to be more reliable trading partners.

Andreas, who had met several other prominent Soviet figures was also struck by the absence of dogma. "With the others, political rhetoric is dominant," Andreas said, "but with this fellow there was no rhetoric and no dogma. It was a very meaty conversation from beginning to end." Andreas added that Gorbachev also seemed surprisingly up-to-date on political affairs in the United States, asking for example how the Soviet Union could make a better impression on American conservatives. Altogether, said Andreas, Gorbachev seemed different from the other Soviet politicians, being more pragmatic and "a working, managerial type."[14]

This assessment was soon to be echoed further afield as Gorbachev embarked on another ambitious foreign visit, this time to Britain. From the time the Aeroflot airliner carrying Gorbachev and his thirty-member delegation touched down at Heathrow airport in bright December sunshine, the Russian was accorded that celebrity status that the British press is so expert in creating. "Mr. G's" every move was charted and explored. But Gorbachev took it all in stride, maintaining a public calm in sometimes trying circumstances.

The timing of the visit had an importance beyond London. It had been announced just previously that the long-stalled negotiations over nuclear weapons would be the subject of discussions in the near future between Foreign Minister

Gromyko and George P. Shultz, the United States Secretary of State. Therefore, Gorbachev's statements on arms control were awaited eagerly, lest they contain hints of policy changes on the part of the Soviet Union. And, from the beginning of his tour, Gorbachev addressed the arms question in surprisingly conciliatory terms. "There are no types of armaments," he said on his arrival, "that the USSR would not agree to see limited and eventually banned in agreement with other states on a reciprocal basis."[15]

Officially Gorbachev was traveling, as he had on the visit eighteen months earlier to Canada, as the head of an interparliamentary delegation. And, again as had been the case in Ottawa, he agreed to appear before the British Parliament's Select Committee on Foreign Relations. Nuclear arms talks were the focus of the statement he made to the committee:

> We still believe that there is and can be no rational alternative to the policy of peaceful coexistence, and I would like to emphasize this point with all certainty.
>
> The Soviet Union remembers perfectly words and deeds which created the climate of mistrust and hostility and destabilized the international situation, but it is not to pique anyone that I am reminding you about that today.
>
> We see our goal in joint settlement of the more important problems which are essentially common for us.
>
> If Britain adheres to this line, we will be glad to cooperate with her. And if the U.S. sticks to this line too and really puts its policy on the track of peaceful cooperation, it will find a reliable partner in ourselves.
>
> I am not going to enumerate all our foreign policy proposals and initiatives here. I want only to say that they envisage the most radical reduction in nuclear armaments—with a view to eventually dismantling them completely—as well as conven-

tional arms, prohibition of chemical weapons, and elimination of their stockpiles.[16]

After a passage emphasizing the Soviet desire to avoid a contest over space weapons, the so-called Star Wars program, Gorbachev went on in a most conciliatory fashion, obviously playing to the Western European anti-nuclear movement, including that in Britain.

> I would like to stress once again that the Soviet leadership stands for forthright and honest talks to help us, on a mutually acceptable basis, limit and reduce arms, primarily nuclear weapons, and eventually eliminate them.
>
> We are ready to go as far as our Western partners in the talks. Naturally enough, equality and equal security shall underlie any agreements in this field. And, of course, any course that seeks military superiority over the USSR and its allies is unacceptable and has no prospects.

Gorbachev then went on to expand on the common nature of the peril that nuclear war posed for all of Europe and to set out the social costs involved in unduly heavy expenditures on the military. He sounded almost like a liberal politician in the West.

> We all agree that ours is a vulnerable, fragile yet interdependent world where we must coexist, whether we want this or not. For all that separates us, we have one planet, and Europe is our common home, not a theater of operations.
>
> The foreign policy of a nation is inseparable from developments on its domestic scene, from its socioeconomic goals and requirements. Our party and state in general emphasize eco-

nomic advance through efficiency and intensive growth factors. We concentrate on the early introduction of the latest
achievements of science and engineering in industry and
agriculture. . . . The Soviet Union needs peace to implement
its huge development programs. . . . [17]

Unlike most Soviet statements made in such surroundings,
Gorbachev's remarks exhibited a certain eloquence. The
usual catchphrases of accepted Marxist-Leninist liturgy
were there, but played down and overtaken by language that
would have stood a Western liberal well. Whether or not this
was Gorbachev's own language, or merely that of a superior
Soviet speechwriter, only the Russians could tell, and they
weren't saying. And that is not to say that this was a peace-
mongering speech. Far from it. Like a very similar statement
he had issued a year previously at the Communist Party
meeting in Portugal, it suggested that the Soviet Union was
flexible on such key issues as arms negotiations but at the
same time it would never allow itself to be put at a disadvan-
tage militarily.

The British accorded their visitor the hospitality normally
reserved for heads of state. One of the highlights was an
elaborate luncheon served in Hampton Court, the Tudor
palace built by Cardinal Wolsey but later appropriated by
Henry VIII. Normally the Great Hall of the palace is a popular tourist venue, but on this occasion it was taken over to fete
the Gorbachevs. Since the hall is without electricity, the soft
lights of candles flickered as the guests dined on poached
salmon, lamb, and chocolate mousse. As another part of their
tourist treatment, Gorbachev and his wife, Raisa, were taken
on a special half-hour tour of Westminster Abbey, the scene of
so much British history. Outside, the Gorbachevs were

heckled by a small group of black-clad women chanting "Free Soviet Jews," but they made no comment. Inside, Gorbachev exhibited the curiosity that many Westerners had commented upon. He paid particular attention to the tombs of Sir Winston Churchill and Charles Darwin and, in a strange aside to the Dean of Westminster, the Very Rev. Edward Carpenter, said: "I feel as if I've been here before."[18]

The following day Gorbachev and his wife, accompanied by key foreign and domestic policy advisers, were the guests of Mrs. Thatcher at Chequers, the British Prime Minister's official country residence. The Gorbachevs, particularly the vivacious, modishly dressed Mrs. Gorbachev, again charmed their hosts. The same reaction was reported in other encounters. For example, one British industrialist, after meeting for two hours with Gorbachev, called him "very humorous and personable." And a British Labor politician was surprised by Mrs. Gorbachev's attempts to conduct a conversation in English about her four-year-old grandchild and found her "a pleasant and charming woman without being shy."[19]

Clearly the most important impression was that which Gorbachev had made on the British Prime Minister. After their Chequers meeting she said: "I like Mr. Gorbachev, we can do business together."[20]

From London, the Gorbachev party moved north to Oxford, where the Russian leader inspected modern, automated automobile factories, giving them the same inquisitive, questioning inspection he had shown elsewhere in similar situations. Then the Gorbachevs headed for Edinburgh and a surprise exhibition of how Mikhail Gorbachev seemed not to be bound by the traditional reservations, if not secretiveness, of the Kremlin.

As reporters gathered around at Edinburgh airport, Gorbachev said somberly: "We have had a great and tragic loss.

The Minister of Defense, our old friend and comrade Dmitri Fyodorovich Ustinov, has passed away." Gorbachev then went on to explain that because of the marshal's death, he was cutting short his visit to Britain and returning to Moscow immediately.[21]

The news was important, but what seemed even more noteworthy was the manner of its announcement. The marshal's death was not being soberly announced by television announcers in Moscow, nor by the official news agency, Tass. Instead, in the relatively obscure airport terminal of an ancient but diplomatically unimportant medium-sized Western city, a high Soviet official merely stated the facts without fuss or fanfare. Gorbachev may have been under some pressure to explain his haste in cutting short a visit that was obviously important to Moscow and which had been going exceedingly well, but such considerations usually did not count with Soviet officials. To the correspondents and diplomats concerned with his visit, it seemed just one more indication of the unusual independence that Gorbachev had achieved in a relatively short period in high office and one more mark of his increasing stature in the Soviet hierarchy.

The death of Marshal Ustinov removed one more major figure from the aging Kremlin leadership. One by one what might be called the post-Stalin, post-Khrushchev leaders had died. First Leonid Brezhnev. Then Mikhail Suslov. Then Yuri Andropov. Now Dmitri Ustinov. And Konstantin Chernenko was obviously in frail health. Only Andrei Gromyko seemed eternal. These men shared a common heritage and a common outlook on events at home and abroad. They may have been too young to play a real role in the Bolshevik Revolution or the civil war that followed, but they were certainly old enough to remember those cataclysmic events. To them the White Guard had been real people and a real threat. Their careers had begun as minor officials in the wake of the horrendous Stalin purges, and their advancement was shaped under the tutelage of such figures as Molotov, Malenkov, and Kuusinen. They had attained high office either just before or during the Khrushchev period, and they had played key roles in removing him from office. With the possible exception of Andropov, they were conservative men, paying lip service to the ideals of Lenin but rigid in their adherence to the dogma of Stalin's state capitalism. Their speeches and writings were full of quotas realized and plans fulfilled but seldom if ever dealt with human emotions or desires. For most of them, increased production required goads, not incentives. They were attached to the status quo, and that was a major reason— although not the only one—why they acted to remove Nikita Khrushchev as general secretary of the party.

Marshal Ustinov probably was less doctrinaire and more a practical man than most of his colleagues. From his origins in the Volga River city of Kuibyshev, through his joining the Red Army as a fourteen-year-old volunteer in 1922, and through a celebrated career as director of munitions plants and military industry he won a reputation as a hard-nosed technocrat. His work in running an arms plant near Leningrad in 1941 drew the thirty-three-year-old Ustinov to the attention of Stalin, who made him People's Commisar for Armaments, the man in charge of producing conventional weapons throughout World War II. He continued in that post for sixteen years, under Stalin and Khrushchev. It was under Leonid Brezhnev that he was eventually promoted to Defense Minister, on the death of Marshal Andrei Grechko in April 1976.

Perhaps the greatest achievement of Marshal Ustinov as a technocrat was the general supervision of the Soviet space program, including the initial orbital flight by Yuri Gagarin. But it would be a mistake to simply classify him as an industrial figure. Especially in the later years of the Brezhnev regime and during the brief Andropov and Chernenko tenures, it was apparently Marshal Ustinov and Foreign Minister Gromyko who provided stability to the Politburo. Now he was dead, and it was easy to understand why Mikhail Gorbachev would describe his passing as a great loss. It was widely believed that the marshal had been a strong supporter of the campaign initiated under Andropov, and with which Gorbachev had become identified, to increase productivity by offering greater incentives to workers and producers.

The marshal's death was not unexpected. He had not been seen in public since late in September and had frequently been reported in poor health. These reports seemed confirmed when he missed the annual commemoration in Red Square of the 1917 Bolshevik Revolution on November 7, 1984. Viktor Grishin, the Politburo member, at that time had sought to minimize the importance of the marshal's absence by saying that he had a "sore throat." Now, once again, as they had so frequently in recent years, the drear rituals of a high Soviet official's funeral would occupy Red Square.

The first indication in Moscow that a high official had died came in an oblique fashion. Authorities announced that a world chess match, already heading for endurance records, would have to be postponed because the Hall of Columns, near Red Square would be required for other purposes. Since that was the usual site for bodies of ranking officials to lie in state, the message was clear.

President Chernenko had gone to the Hall of Columns to pay tribute to the dead Defense Minister. But the day of the funeral was bitterly cold, with the temperature hovering just below zero, and there was no sign of Chernenko for the ceremonies in Red Square. As a frozen mist shrouded the great open square, a black- and red-draped gun carriage carried the urn bearing the marshal's ashes toward the burial place in the Kremlin wall. Leading the cortege was Mikhail Gorbachev, along with Grigory Romanov, chairman of the funeral commission. As frozen troops cautiously stomped their feet and chafed their faces to keep warm, Romanov delivered the main funeral oration. Other speakers included Grishin and Marshal Sergei Sokolov, Marshal Ustinov's newly named successor as Defense Minister.[22]

The choice of Marshal Sokolov had created a mild surprise in Moscow. When Romanov was named chairman of the Ustinov funeral commission, there was widespread belief that in view of previous Soviet practice that would mean that he would become the new Defense Minister. Marshal Ustinov had filled a similar role for his predecessor, Marshal Grechko, who in turn had supervised the funeral arrangements for his predecessor, Marshal Rodion Malinovsky. There was good precedent to support the supposition that tradition would count in other ways, too. Marshal Ustinov himself, although he had held a reserve military rank for years, was more civilian than soldier. Romanov, with years of experience in directing military industries in Leningrad would therefore have seemed a natural choice to maintain civilian control over the military apparatus, always a necessary ingredient of Soviet politics.

Some months earlier, the choice might have been still different. At that time the most prominent military figure in the country was the outspoken Marshal Nikolai Ogarkov. Beetle-browed Ogarkov had forced his way into the consciousness of the Western world at the time of his press conference to try to explain the Soviet rationale for shooting down the South Korean airliner. But he had reportedly been a source of friction in the Soviet military establishment long before that. He made no secret of the fact that he wanted a greater share of the Soviet budget for military expenditures, and he was seen as strongly anti-Western in his views. Such opinions could quite well have also antagonized Gorbachev and his like-minded colleagues in the Politburo who wanted the state's rubles for other development projects. There were even reports that Marshal Ustinov, already aware that he was fatally ill, acted to make sure that Ogarkov was not in a position to succeed him. Whatever the reason, in September 1984, Ogarkov was abruptly relieved as the Red Army's Chief of Staff. His new appointment was not publicly disclosed but was believed to be as a field commander on the Western European frontier. He was present in Moscow for Marshal Ustinov's lying-in-state but was positioned out of the limelight in the secondary rows of military officers.

It is also possible that the Ogarkov ouster was connected to a diplomatic change of attitude that seemed to be apparent in Moscow at this time. Gorbachev's conciliatory speeches during the visit to Britain may have been part of the same campaign, as well might have been a subdued statement Chernenko distributed through Dr. Armand Hammer, the American businessman who has had dealings with all the Soviet leaders since Lenin. But the net result was that Secretary Shultz and Foreign Minister Gromyko did meet in Geneva, and the cold war of hot words subsided on both sides.

In Moscow Gorbachev and Romanov apparently had divided the areas of responsibility in the Politburo and the Secretariat. Romanov, as pointed out earlier, was in charge of the military-industrial apparatus. He shared with Gorbachev the work of overseeing the administrative bureaucracy. But Gorbachev had charge of ideology, even though he lacked the obvious qualifications in the way of speeches and writings that normally go with the portfolio. In addition he supervised the party apparatus and the cadres, and he had charge of the whole economic program including agriculture and light industry. His influence extended throughout most key areas of the party and the administration, including several where

Romanov was the nominal superior. In the ideological area, Gorbachev had three junior Central Committee secretaries working under him. They were Mikhail Zimyanin, who had charge of domestic ideological matters; the elderly Boris Ponomarev and Konstantin Rusakov, who dealt with questions of Communism abroad. In the industrial area, two "junior" secretaries of the Central Committee reported to Gorbachev. In charge of economic matters was Nikolai Ryshkov and at the head of the light industry departments was Gorbachev's old friend Ivan Kapitonov. The "junior" secretary for heavy industry, Vladimir Dolgikh, reported to Romanov.[23]

During much of this time, Chernenko had seldom been seen in public. And when he had, the evidence of his frailty was unmistakable. For example, it was reported that when he had gone to the Bolshoi Ballet on one occasion, a "human chair" of aides had been required to carry him up the stairs to the official loge. In addition, a special meeting of Warsaw Pact leaders scheduled to have been held in Sofia was canceled, and Soviet officials did not conceal that Chernenko's poor health had been the reason. Then, in the middle of February 1985, the Greek Prime Minister Andreas Papandreou visited Moscow. Tikhonov and other high officials tendered him an elaborate reception, but Chernenko was apparently too ill to join the proceedings.

Once more, and again after the briefest of intervals, the Kremlin prepared for a change of leadership. But this time, the change seemed more significant. This time a generational switch was involved. One by one, the Stalin generation of party leaders had held on to the end, but now they were giving way to a new group. And most prominent in that group was Mikhail Sergeyevich Gorbachev, the determined young man from Stavropol.

6

Tying
the
Strings
Together

THE SOVIET Union is without doubt, in strategic terms, a superpower. Its military might is by most reckonings second only to that of the United States, despite stories told about distrust and unrest in the lower ranks of its armed forces. Its political influence is felt around the world and in many places challenges the Western democracies for hegemony. It is also a significant factor in world trade, but its internal economics are problem-ridden. Some of those problems have persisted or indeed worsened for years.

The Soviet political and governmental system is much more complex than that of most Western countries. To understand the dimension of the problems facing Gorbachev, it is necessary to know how the Soviet Union operates and how it has changed over the years. In simple terms, the Communist Party rules, and within the Communist Party the most powerful office is that of the general secretary. His preeminence stems from the fact that he is the chairman of two powerful institutions: the Politburo and the secretariat of the Central

Committee of the party. The Politburo is a small group, usually about twelve voting members plus some candidate, or nonvoting members, charged with directing the work of the party between plenary sessions of the Central Committee, which in normal times are held twice a year. Nominally members of the Politburo are elected by the Central Committee, but in fact since the time of Stalin they have been coopted by either the general secretary, if he is powerful enough, or by the collective Politburo when a vacancy occurs. Some members of the Politburo, in addition to the general secretary, are also members of the secretariat. This double positioning gives them great power.

The Central Committee secretaries not only supervise the operations of the party apparatus, but they oversee the departments of the Central Committee itself. The Central Committee is also nominally elected at party congresses but, as in the case of the Politburo, its members are largely coopted by the general secretary or the Politburo members if they have enough clout. Normally the Central Committee consists of about three hundred voting members, plus, like the Politburo, some candidate or nonvoting members. Departments of the Central Committee—about twenty in all—cover both supervision of party work and purely governmental functions. The Central Committee's Department for Science and Education, for example, as part of its function would supervise the state Ministry of Education plus many other government bodies.

The government ministries themselves are many and varied. They are supervised on a day-to-day basis by members of the Council of Ministers, who technically are named by the Supreme Soviet, the nation's parliament, at its first session after its election. In practice, the process here is the same as for the Politburo and the Central Committee.

Whoever runs the party, whether it be one general secretary or a collective of members of the Politburo, names the chairman of the Council of Ministers (often called the Premier) and the other ministers.

The Supreme Soviet itself is elected at five-year intervals by all Soviet citizens over the age of eighteen. In practice, since only one slate of candidates approved by the Communist Party is offered, the election is controlled by the party leadership.

Gorbachev has made his way to the top of this complex structure and from that position he will have to deal with a host of political and economic problems. The most serious economic problem, and the one with which Gorbachev has been most closely identified, is the fact that the Soviet Union seems chronically unable to feed the quarter of a billion people, or more, who live within its borders. As has already been outlined, this is due to a number of factors, some of which are not really within man's ability to control. But other difficulties are truly man-made—inefficiency, corruption, laziness, ignorance—and that is where Gorbachev had already directed his efforts in such experiments as that with his Pyatigorsk kolkhoz.

Some foreign analysts have serious doubts that one strong-willed man can make a difference in the way the Soviet economy behaves. They see the fundamental problem as being more political than economic and until there is a sea change in the politics of the Kremlin, they doubt that there can be a change for the better in industrial and agricultural production.

Leonard Schapiro, the well-known British historian and political analyst, put it this way: "Though the method of government has changed enormously, its basic mechanism is the same, because no new institutions have taken the place of the old."[1] What Schapiro meant was that although the heinous purges and inhuman five-year development plans of the Stalin era had been softened, the same political structure with its components—the Communist Party, the KGB and other police bodies, and the military—have remained in place. Each of those components has held jealously to what it considered its fair share of the fruits of socialist toil, becoming ever more conservative and showing ever less initiative as the years went by.

Professor Seweryn Bialer of Columbia University has expressed a similar view. "Unless the Soviets make major changes in their economic system," he said, "they will be in a state of internal decline, but this doesn't mean they'll disintegrate. It simply means that the system is becoming less effective, that the leaders will act piecemeal, making policy and administrative reforms but not structural reforms. In this way, the reforms will not change the system; the system will absorb the reforms. And in this situation, we can say that hard times produce hard lines."[2]

The veteran Canadian diplomat, Robert Ford, who served in Moscow for twenty years between 1946 and 1980, has expressed a slightly different view. "From 1918 on," he wrote, "the Soviet leaders have seldom hesitated in choosing a pragmatic course over the rigid application of ideology, and there is ample justification in Lenin's writing for doing so. There is no reason to believe the next set of leaders will be any less pragmatic in either foreign or domestic affairs. Yet it must be realized that all of them will have come up through the Party apparatus, possibly having spent some time in the practical administration of large industrial or agricultural enterprises, but all deeply in debt to the Party for their promotion to the good life and for the perquisites, influence, and power which put members of the nomenklatura in a new and highly privileged class. Their prime aim will be to maintain and consolidate this gratifying situation."[3]

The common strand in all these ideas is inertia. The high-sounding phrases of Lenin's revolution no longer can arouse a population that has heard them in factory floor speeches, has heard them from Komsomol organizers like young Mikhail Gorbachev at Moscow University, has seen them on street corner billboards, and recited them from primary school textbooks all their lives. Thus, when a Western passenger on an Aeroflot flight from Moscow to Odessa inquires of his seatmate, a young woman from Khabarovsk on her way to a seaside vacation, what the stewardess had said about "the Hero City of Kiev," she retorts with some impatience: "O, don't pay attention to that. That's just propaganda." The promises of a better future in return for harder work have been made too often without fulfillment. There is no incentive to achieve, to advance, so why bother.

Nowhere is this more applicable than in agriculture. True, a great deal of the Soviet Union's difficulties in producing enough grain, meat, and butter stem from the nation's inhospitable climate, lack of enough fertile soil or water or sun, but another problem has been the simple lack of interest on the part of the rural work force to increase production beyond the bare quotas set by the central planning authority.

The figures speak for themselves. In 1978, the year that Gorbachev took over direction of the Soviet agriculture apparatus, the grain harvest set a record total of 235 million tons. In the following six years, the harvest did not nearly approach that record, mostly hovering around 180 million to 190 million tons, the estimated total for 1984. To make up the difference between domestic supply and demand, the Russians are forced to import about 40 million tons each year from Canada, Australia, Argentina, France, and, of course, the United States.[4]

Gorbachev was the man in charge during those six years, but he escaped the criticism and ignominy that befell his predecessors in the agriculture portfolio. A certain amount of luck, bad and good, obviously has been involved. Some bad luck has involved the weather, too dry in the growing season, too wet at harvest time. Some good luck, from Gorbachev's point of view, has been the fact that the rapid succession of leadership crises that paralleled his custody of the agriculture apparatus has probably diverted some of the attention from the apparatus's shortcomings. But, beyond those considerations, from conversations with such people as Eugene Whalen and Dwayne Andreas, Gorbachev has let it be known that he is not overly interested in short-term rallies in grain production. He seeks a substantive revision of the Soviet Union's agricultural aims. In other words he would avoid the quick-cure programs such as Khrushchev's Virgin Lands development scheme, perhaps by shifting the areas devoted to grain production to much more amenable climatic zones.

That is why the huge land reclamation program announced by Chernenko at the Central Committee plenum in October 1984 would seem to have Gorbachev's blessing. At the plenum, Tikhonov filled in the details. He said the reasons for the program were basic: 70 percent of the agricultural land in the Soviet Union lacks sufficient rainfall; the bulk of the rest gets too much. By reclaiming land that was too wet but with otherwise the proper climate, and by providing irrigation to dry areas, the plan was designed to place at least half of the nation's grain crop outside weather risks. Tikhonov reported that, between 1966 and 1984, reclaimed land had increased from 42 million to 82 million acres but between 1984 and 2000 it was hoped to increase the total to 131 million acres. He also said that the bulk of the program would be directed at the warmer areas in the south of the Soviet Union.[5]

But getting enough land in the proper setting is not the only answer to solving the Soviet Union's food difficulties. Dealing with the inertia on the state and collective farms is perhaps just as important. Stalin, through his proxies Malenkov and Khrushchev, tried to solve that problem by establishing machine tractor stations whose personnel informed on malingering, sometimes even where none existed. Khrushchev tried to improve the lot of the rural population by developing agro-towns where the farm workers would have all the facilities available to the city workers. Brezhnev rolled back Khrushchev's policies but did not really replace them with anything beyond exhortation until May 1982, when he announced his new food program, probably with Gorbachev's backing. That program called for more efficient management, better machinery, decentralized planning, and greater incentives.

Gorbachev was not making idle chatter in those plants in southern Ontario; he really wanted to know what motivated the Canadian workers to produce so much better than their counterparts in the Soviet Union. Gorbachev knows the figures that suggest that much can be done if the farmers are motivated.[6] But the question is what will motivate the Soviet farmers to work as hard on the state land as on their own? Gorbachev has already suggested he knows part of the answer, better living conditions, more consumer goods, more tangible rewards. It may sound a little like Khrushchev's agro-towns in retrospect, but to a family living in conditions that have barely improved in the nearly seven decades since the revolution, that is of no consequence. Rural electrification is just as well received in the Soviet Union as it was in the Tennessee Valley.

Whatever the problems of Soviet agriculture, they are much the same as those troubling Soviet industry. Distortions in planning produce goods with little relation to the reality of the demand. For example, it has been estimated that factories in the Soviet Union produce one hundred and thirty different makes of refrigerators, seventy different vacuum cleaners, fifty-six kinds of television sets, forty sewing machines, and even thirty kinds of electric razors. On the face of it, that would seem to offer the Soviet consumer an enviable choice of product. But the fact of the matter is that of those one hundred and thirty refrigerator types, most are hopelessly out of date and those that aren't probably aren't available for the average purchaser. The output of the refrigerator plant is geared to the producer, not to the consumer.[7]

Quality control is also a major headache in Soviet industry. Many stories are told in Soviet cities about how it is wise to buy a television set that was made in the first half of the month (supposedly the timing can be deciphered from the number of the set) because the workers assembling it will still be working at their normal leisurely pace and will not be rushing pell mell to complete the quota that threatens to slip away from them toward the end of the month. Some one who had heard such stories would appreciate the uniformly good quality of Canadian butter.

And quality is not the only irritant. Many goods, especially those too small or too simple to require elaborate planning, tend not to be available at all. When they do show up, long lines of shoppers instantly form seeking the aspirin, toothbrushes, shoe polish, detergent, or other household items that American consumers waste with such abandon.[8]

Gorbachev himself has spoken about the need for improvement. In his 1983 appearance before the parliamentary committee in Ottawa, he said: "Industrial growth rates have in recent years not suited us. They have been lower than those on which we counted, but I must say that as a result of measures which have been taken and which cover a wide range of problems—matters of production organization, cooperation between industrial enterprises, labor incentive, tightening up labor discipline, and improving planning work—have now enabled us to improve the situation somewhat. . . ."[9]

If Gorbachev is to make serious inroads in solving—or at least in easing—these problems, he must first tackle the question of changing the way the party and the system works. Needless to say, that will not be easy, although he does have some things working for him, not least the age factor. Leonid Brezhnev came to power because the party reacted to what it saw as the dangerous adventurism of Nikita Khrushchev. To the estimated 100,000 senior party and bureaucratic officials (they are not always the same thing) anything that smacks of change carries a threat to their well-being and therefore can be classified as adventurism. But quite apart from their inherent danger for do-nothing bureaucrats, it is easy to say that many of Khrushchev's proposals were ill-considered. However, it is less easy to say that ending them was the right approach, from the viewpoint of the Soviet citizen. How else can be explained the apparent satisfaction so many of the Russian people have expressed with the shakeup that Yuri Andropov promised and the regret of those same Russian people that he did not live long enough to pursue his aims.

In the West, particularly in the English-speaking countries, the concept of democracy that includes government and loyal opposition, tends to warp views of other peoples' expectations. The Soviet Union—Russia—has no such tradition. Marxism-Leninism is merely a new branch grafted on the autocratic tree first nurtured by the royal Romanovs. To the average Russian, it often seems that the country runs best when it has a strong leader with a deliberate course of action in mind. Of course no one would opt for the murderous purges of a Stalin or the sometimes equally deadly schemes of a Peter the Great, but few Russians would question that both those tyrants achieved greatness for their people and their nation. So, when an Andropov, seemingly a stern but probably honest leader, arrived in the Kremlin, there was genuine appreciation among the Russians.

Is Gorbachev a strong enough personality to bring about a significant shift in popular attitudes in the Soviet Union? To answer that question, it is first necessary to consider certain changes that have occurred in Moscow's domains. Perhaps the most important of those changes is that for the first time, the average Ivan Ivanovich has some real knowledge of how the outside world lives. Through television, and to a lesser extent through printed materials, through experiences related by people who have traveled abroad—and they are a significant number—and through meeting foreigners who visit the Soviet Union, he has shaped perceptions that allow him to measure the progress of the Soviet Union against that of the outside world. What he sees usually does not please him although sometimes the reaction is muted by that narrow Russian (or Ukrainian) chauvinism that still persists. But at other times it erupts in strikes and demonstrations over food shortages such as that which affected the Togliatti and other car plants in the 1980s or the near riots that affected Odessa earlier over the shipping of food to Cuba while the families of the local dock workers in the great Black Sea port were going hungry. But since the perception exists, it can be harnessed as a prod to more diligent labor. In other words, the Soviet people can be told that if you work hard enough you too can have a nice car or a nice apartment or a nice vacation in Prague. The trouble with such a scenario, from the Communist Party's point of view, is that it requires a major relaxation of controls—or greater liberty, if you will—for the Soviet people. The example of Yugoslavia comes readily to mind, and it is not one that Mikhail Gorbachev might be expected to emulate.

As his testy reply to the British Member of Parliament who questioned him about human rights in the Soviet Union would indicate, Gorbachev seems to have strong views about how laws should operate in his homeland. Lawbreakers—and, to a man like Gorbachev, a dissenter is a lawbreaker—deserve the punishments they get. He could not have won the support and patronage of men like Mikhail Suslov and Yuri Andropov if he thought otherwise.

But, from what he says and what he suggests, it seems likely that he would move toward some opening in the direction of greater economic, if not political, freedom. In other words, he must seek to sponsor initiative while at the same time preventing license. And that is where the age factor could be of assistance. To make such changes it would be necessary to make sweeping alterations in the makeup of the bodies of authority through which the party governs, principally the Central Committee and the various ministries of the government. Time is on Gorbachev's side. Leonid Brezhnev, opting for the serenity of the known, rather than the possible turbulence of the unknown, made few changes in the upper reaches of the party and its various organs. Yuri Andropov may have wanted to make changes, and with Gorbachev's help some were initiated, but generally the status remained quo. Under Konstantin Chernenko, the changes continued but still slowly.

The result of this resistance to change has meant that many of the higher officials are of pensionable age or beyond. The trend that has removed Kosygin, Suslov, Brezhnev, Andropov, Ustinov, Pelshe, and the others from the Politburo by death is also evident in the lesser offices. The 1980s proved a severe test for the Soviet political system. The seemingly endless period that was spent waiting for Leonid Brezhnev either to retire or resign, the sudden ascension and death of Andropov and then the twilight time of Chernenko were episodes that challenged the system in a way that it had not been confronted previously. It brought into the open the question of how succession to power in the Kremlin is regulated and showed that the party, even after seven decades, has not really dared to face up to it until now.

Because of the recent events, however, the realization would seem to have penetrated that the leaders of a modern superpower can no longer function like the boyars who put Mikhail Romanov on the throne in 1613. Gorbachev will have this realization working for him, and it should help him name his own people to take the places of the departing oldsters. To a certain extent, he was able to achieve some of the changes required after he became the Central Committee secretary in charge of personnel.

Robert Ford relates an ancedote that illustrates the difficulty of making improvements, not only because of the resistance to change, but also because of the peculiar traditions of the Soviet state and party. Ford once asked a senior member of the Central Committee why Arvid Pelshe, then aged eighty-three, was still a member of the Politburo. The Russian looked at Ford in surprise and said: "Why, he is the only one who knew Lenin."[10]

142

But not all the high officials of the Soviet Union are tottering octogenarians. What about men such as Grigory Romanov and Vitaly Vorotnikov, men of Gorbachev's own age? Would they support drastic overhauls of the economy and the party?

It is almost impossible to ascertain the true relationship between the highest officials of the Soviet Union. But from the meager evidence available it seems highly likely that Gorbachev and Romanov have already worked out an arrangement that suits them. Others, like Vorotnikov, have much in common with Gorbachev's apparent aims and, perhaps more important, they belong to the same new elite, they enjoy the same privileged status, and they doubtless would like to keep it that way. They have resented the Brezhnev era officials, feeling that they clung to power long after they should have gone gracefully into retirement.

These people also share different backgrounds from the Brezhnev group; generally, like Gorbachev, they were too young to be involved in Stalin's, or even Khrushchev's, programs to any great extent. They have no memory of the revolution or the civil war. They take as normal such creature comforts as a reasonable-sized apartment, a television set, or even a car—things that were novelties to the Brezhnev generation.[11] Ideology means less to them as well. This is reflected in many ways. By speeches they make at party gatherings, where studies have shown that the younger officials tend to speak less about ideology and more about economic and social subjects. It is also reflected on occasions such as that in London where Gorbachev omitted a scheduled visit to Karl Marx's grave to lay a wreath and sent an aide instead, or when Gorbachev can crack a joke to the British that they "can blame the British Museum for Karl Marx."

On a personal level, there does seem to be a connection between Gorbachev and Vorotnikov, dating to their service in the Caucasus. It was probably not by chance that Gorbachev was the person who nominated Vorotnikov for the position as chairman of the Council of Ministers of the Russian republic in June 1983.

There are, of course, some storm clouds on the horizon that could upset the future plans of Gorbachev and his associates. One of the more important of these is the swiftly changing population makeup of the Soviet Union. In the 1979 census, Russians proper numbered 137.4 million, just over half of the 262.1 million total. Other Slavs, principally Ukrainians and Byelorussians, numbered about 52 million more. But the numbers of the non-Russians, non-Slavs are growing at a much faster rate. In the R.S.F.S.R., where naturally by far the greatest portion of the population is ethnic Russian, for example, the birth rate in 1979 was 18.2 per 1,000. In the Tadzhik S.S.R., however, the birth rate was 37.5 per 1,000.[12] This population trend has not yet been reflected in the makeup of the Communist Party, but the pressure can be expected for changes to be made. Up to now, the Politburo has usually contained a token representative of the Kazakhs or Uzbeks, and universities have admitted a limited quota of students from those ethnic groups. But in the near future greater attention will have to be paid to them. Gorbachev, coming from the polyglot Caucasus, although from a Russian background, might be expected to be more sympathetic to the aspirations of the non-Russian Soviet citizens than earlier Soviet leaders, including the Georgian turned Great Russian chauvinist, Stalin.

The racial question is not limited merely to ethnic origin. Religion also plays a significant part in the lives of many Soviet citizens beyond the Urals, specifically Islam. According to some reports, this factor has already proved a problem in Afghanistan where Moslem soldiers of the Red Army have been reported reluctant to act against their co-religionists, the Afghan rebels. Religious, or what might better be termed cultural-religious, trends from outside the Soviet Union can create effects within the country too. The Islamic revolution of Ayatollah Khomeini certainly contained many such warning signs for the Soviet leadership.

If the present trends continue, these questions are bound to prove nettlesome for the men in the Kremlin for the ancient fears and hatreds of the Russians, subjugated for so long by the Golden Horde, still lie ominously close to the surface in the Soviet Union. This is expressed in various ways but nowhere more pathetically than in the uprooting of the Crimean Tatar population during World War II and their continued diaspora nearly half a century later despite promises from Andropov, among others, that justice would be done.

These are matters of domestic concern. In foreign affairs, too, changes seem almost certain.

In its seven decades, the Soviet Union has had remarkably few Foreign Ministers: Georgi Chicherin, Maxim Litvinov, Vyacheslav Molotov, Andrei Vishinsky, Dmitri Shepilov, and Andrei Gromyko are in effect the only incumbents. Gromyko's tenure at or near the pinnacle of the Soviet Foreign Office is most notable. He entered the service when Litvinov was in charge and Gorbachev was a child. He served under Stalin, Khrushchev, Brezhnev, Andropov, and Chernenko. He was part of the Soviet establishment during the Nazi-Soviet Pact, through World War II, through the founding of the United Nations, through the Korean, Vietnam, and various Middle East Wars. He fought the Cold War as well. He is the last of his generation, the Stalin generation, to occupy a seat on the Politburo. It is doubtful that his kind will be seen again.

The reasons are simple. In the time of Litvinov, Molotov, and Vishinsky, the Soviet Union was ruled by Stalin, a man suspicious of the outside world, not comfortable in alien surroundings, and willing, if not eager, to have someone else run errands for him. Khrushchev, it is true, and Brezhnev, in the early years of his term, were willing to travel abroad and to conduct diplomatic negotiations, but they too left most of that kind of work to Gromyko. Andropov and Chernenko's terms were so relatively brief that foreign policy was left almost entirely up to Gromyko.

Gromyko's longevity also gave him domestic political power that had been largely denied to his predecessors, with the exception of Molotov at various stages of the Stalin era and early in Khrushchev's reign. He, in fact, may have eventually become a kingmaker in alliance with Defense Minister Ustinov in the case of both Andropov and Chernenko. There is no reason to believe that his successor would carry the same political clout.

Gorbachev, moreover, is quite different from previous Soviet leaders. His foreign travels have brought him into contact first of all with the Communist parties of most of the major countries of Europe, East and West, on their home grounds. In addition, he has been to Mongolia and Vietnam, to Britain and North America. He seems to delight in new surroundings, his inquisitive nature finding full play in seeing and experiencing novelties. Gorbachev has had the opportunity to see how Western democracies function. In Ottawa, for example, he sat beaming in the Visitors Gallery of the House of Commons while Prime Minister Trudeau was roasted by opposition critics for an interview in which he had criticized the policies of President Reagan. Even Trudeau's response that he had told Gorbachev that "some of the statements by *Pravda* or some of the Soviet leaders about the Americans are excessive and not conducive to peaceful negotiations," failed to assuage the critics.[13] Moreover, the priorities Gorbachev seems likely to set for the Soviet Union would seem to assume stability in dealings with foreign nations. To trade, you have to talk.

But Gorbachev is not likely to be an easy trading partner, and he is likely to suit his foreign policy to his business aims. His conversation with Dwayne Andreas showed that clearly; unless the possibility of a trade embargo could be completely ruled out, he simply would shop somewhere else. Age is also a factor in the Soviet foreign service. Key men like Gromyko, Ambassador Anatoly Dobrynin in Washington, and others would seem to be nearing the end of their service. There are several likely replacements, among them Leonid Zamyatin, a veteran foreign service official who has already accompanied Gorbachev on some of his travels.

Like the Soviet Union, several of the Eastern European nations have aging leaderships that soon must depart. Men like Janos Kadar, Todor Zhivkov, and others have been in power for long periods, much in the way that Leonid Brezhnev was in Moscow. And, even more than the Russian people, the citizens of the satellite countries have increasingly rising expectations about their standards of living. They have much greater access to knowledge about the affluence of Western society. And they want to share in it. And already there is some resentment in the Soviet Union that the Hungarians and the Czechs seem to enjoy a better standard of living than their Russian friends. If the gap were to widen, it would create new tensions for the rulers in the Kremlin. But, among Moscow's allies, the greatest question of all still hangs over Warsaw. As Gorbachev was rising in the Kremlin, General Jaruzelski had tamed some of the rebellion in Poland. But even more than in the Soviet Union, the Polish people and the Communist party have come to realize that the system does not really work well or fairly. When persistent criticism by the Roman Catholic church is added to that social mixture it becomes extremely volatile.

Another area of great uncertainty with which Gorbachev must deal is the military. As in all other areas of the Soviet leadership, age is a crucial factor in the military command. Defense Minister Sergei Sokolov was seventy-three when he took over the role, following the death of Marshal Ustinov. Marshal Ogarkov was sixty-seven when he was demoted at about the same time. Others in the high command are of the same age, men who served as younger officers in World War II and just before. In some cases, like the Brezhnev era politicians of similar age, they benefited from Stalin's infamous military purges that led to the deaths of thousands of military officers almost on the eve of the German invasion. At the time of Marshal Ustinov's death, there was considerable speculation that Grigory Romanov might be named to succeed him. That didn't happen, but Romanov, through his supervision of the heavy, defense-related industries, will continue to have a major say in the military's welfare. For this reason alone, it will be important to Gorbachev to stay on good terms with him. Not that Gorbachev is without some clout himself. In what might be called his Suslov guise, he controls the political administration throughout the military and the security organs.

To tie all these strings together will take considerable political sleight of hand. It will also take a great deal of driving determination to achieve the improvement in their living conditions that the great silent majority of the Soviet people have made clear they want. By his swift rise from the obscurity of Stavropol, accomplished with such remarkable agility that he has been linked to most of the senior Soviet officials of the 1970s and '80s, Gorbachev must be considered a politician of unusual ability. Those who have known him also stress that determination to achieve his ambitions has always been a hallmark of his personality. Fate has been kind to Mikhail Gorbachev so far. Whether it will continue to be so, only time will tell.

Acknowledgments and Explanations

Only history can give a definitive verdict on Mikhail Sergeyevich Gorbachev, but in writing this book I have endeavored to explain why, seemingly out of nowhere, a radically different kind of Soviet leader has emerged.

Of course, given the traditional secrecy of the Moscow apparatus, there are gaps in the story as I have compiled it. For those and any errors I take full responsibility.

Many people have helped in the hurried and harried work of piecing this biography together. My colleagues at *The New York Times*, as always, have been cooperative and encouraging. I pay special thanks to Theodore Shabad, Jeanne Pinder, and David Binder, but there are others as well.

Further afield, my old friend Robert Johnstone of the Canadian Broadcasting Corp. helped provide material from Canada. Eduardo Gaitan Rojo helped with the Portuguese material.

The staffs of the Slavonic Division, New York Public Library, and at the Bibliotheque de Documentation Internationale Contemporaine, University of Paris, at Nanterre, were unfailingly helpful.

I would also like to thank Frederich and Lidia Nieznansky, Mrs. Zoya Golinskaya, Eugene Koniev, and "Irene" for sharing with me their recollections of the younger Gorbachev or his youthful environment. In this regard, Valery Golovskoy was also particularly helpful.

Jerry F. Hough, the American scholar who was probably the first to start tracking Gorbachev's rise to power, offered some helpful advice. Nicholas Mango, of Columbia University's Harriman Institute, was a fast and efficient translator.

The enthusiasm of Sol Stein and Patricia Day has been a constant source of encouragement.

Finally, this book would not have been possible without the assistance of Elizabeth Margaritis Butson, who acted as editor, researcher, gofer, and cheerleader. The book is dedicated to her and to my children, Alexander, Tom, Miles, and Jennifer.

Bibliography

Andropov, Yuri V. *Speeches and Writings*. Elmsford, N.Y.: Pergamon Press, 1983.

Beichman, Arnold and Bernstam, Mikhail. *Andropov, New Challenge to the West*. New York: Stein and Day, 1983.

Bialer, Seweryn. *Stalin's Successors: Leadership, Stability and Change in the Soviet Union*. Cambridge: Cambridge University Press, 1980.

Blackwell, Robert E., Jr. "Cadres Policy in the Brezhnev Era." In *Problems of Communism*, March-April, 1979. Vol. XXVIII. Washington, D.C., 1979.

Bromke, Adam. "The Andropov Succession: East-West Relations in the 1980's." In *Behind the Headlines*. Toronto: Canadian Institute of International Affairs, 1983.

Brown, Archie. "Andropov: Discipline and Reform." In *Problems of Communism*, January-February, 1983. Vol. XXXII. Washington, D.C., 1983.

Chernenko, M., ed. *Idyet Voina Narodnaya 1941-45*. Stavropol: Kniga Izdatelstvestva, 1967.

Colton, Timothy J. *The Dilemma of Reform in the Soviet Union.* New York: Council on Foreign Relations, 1984.

Conquest, Robert. *Russia After Khrushchev.* New York: Praeger, 1965.

_____ *The Great Terror.* New York: Macmillan, 1968.

Dornberg, John. *The New Tsars: Russia Under Stalin's Heirs.* Garden City, N.Y.: Doubleday, 1972.

_____ *Brezhnev: The Masks of Power.* New York: Basic Books, 1974.

Ebon, Martin. *The Andropov File.* New York: McGraw-Hill, 1983.

Ford, Robert A. "The Next Soviet Decade." In *Foreign Policy,* Summer 1984. Vol. 62, No. 5. New York, 1984.

Frankland, Mark. *Khrushchev.* New York: Stein and Day, 1967.

Gelb, Leslie H. "What We Really Know About Russia." In *The New York Times Magazine,* Oct. 24, 1984. New York.

Gelman, Harry. *The Brezhnev Politburo and the Decline of Detente.* Ithaca, N.Y. and London: Cornell University Press, 1984.

Gidwitz, Betsy. "Labor Unrest in the Soviet Union." In *Problems of Communism,* November-December, 1982. Vol. XXXI. Washington, D.C., 1982.

Grechko, Marshal A. A. *Bitva za Kavkaz.* Moscow: Voennoe Izdatelstvo Ministerstva Oboroni SSSR, 1967.

Hough, Jerry F. "Andropov's First Year." In *Problems of Communism,* November-December, 1983. Vol. XXXII. Washington, D.C., 1983.

_____ *Soviet Leadership in Transition.* Washington, D.C.: The Brookings Institution, 1980.

_____ and Ploss, Sidney I. "Signs of Struggle." In *Problems of Communism,* September-October, 1982. Vol. XXXI. Washington, D.C., 1982.

Hyland, William G. "Kto Kogo in the Kremlin." In *Problems of Communism*, January-February, 1982. Vol. XXXI. Washington, D.C., 1982.

Leonhard, Wolfgang. *Nikita Sergueievitch Khrouchtchev: Ascension et Chute d'un Homme d'Etat Sovietique.* Lausanne: Editions Rencontre, 1965.

Medvedev, Roy. *Khrushchev.* Garden City, N.Y.: Anchor Press/Doubleday, 1983.

Medvedev, Zhores A. *Andropov.* New York: W. W. Norton, 1983.

Rahr, Alexander G. *A Biographic Directory of 100 Leading Soviet Officials.* Munich: Central Research, Radio Liberty, 1984.

Rigby, T. H. "The Soviet Regional Leadership: the Brezhnev Generation." In *Slavic Review.* Vol. 37, No. 1. March, 1978. Urbana, Ill., 1978.

Rositzke, Harry. *The KGB: The Eyes of Russia.* Garden City, N.Y.: Doubleday, 1981.

Rush, Myron. *Political Succession in the USSR.* New York: Columbia University Press, 1967.

Shevchenko, Arkady N. *Breaking With Moscow.* New York: Alfred A. Knopf, 1985.

Solovyov, Vladimir and Klepikova, Elena. *Yuri Andropov— A Secret Passage Into the Kremlin.* New York: Macmillan, 1983.

Steele, Jonathan and Abraham, Eric. *Andropov in Power.* Garden City, N.Y.: Anchor Press/Doubleday, 1984.

Tatu, Michel. *Power in the Kremlin.* Translated by Helen Katel. New York: Viking, 1968.

Taubman, William. "Moscow U: Dialectics Is a Drag." In *Saturday Review*, Feb. 17, 1968. New York.

Ulam, Adam B. *Stalin: The Man and His Era.* New York: Viking, 1973.

Voslensky, Michael. *Nomenklatura: The Soviet Ruling Class —An Insider's Report.* Translated by Eric Mosbacher. Garden City, N.Y.: Doubleday, 1984.
Zemtsov, Ilia. *Andropov: Politicheskie Dilemmi i Borba Vlast.* Jerusalem: Vinitsky, 1983.

Notes

1

1. *Minutes of Proceedings and Evidence of the Standing Committee on External Affairs and National Defense.* Issue No. 95, May 17, 1983. Queen's Printer, Ottawa.
2. *New York Times, The,* December 19, 1984.
3. *Daily Telegraph,* London, December 22, 1984.
4. *New York Times, The,* December 14, 1984.
5. *New York Times, The,* November 22, 1984.
6. *Financial Times,* London, December 19, 1984.
7. *New York Times, The,* March 1, 1984.
8. Andropov, Y. V., *Speeches and Writings* (Oxford: Pergamon Press, 1983), p. 186.

2

1. Grechko, Marshal A. A., *Bitva za Kavkaz* (Moscow: Voennoe Izdatelstvo Ministerstva Oboroni SSSR, 1967) pp 60-62; Interview with Hon. Eugene Whalen.
2. Interview with "Irene."
3. Interview with Frederich and Lidia Nieznansky; Taubman, William: "Moscow U: Dialectics Is a Drag," in *Saturday Review*, February 17, 1968.
4. Ibid.
5. Nieznansky interview.
6. Hough, Jerry F.: "Andropov's First Year," in *Problems of Communism*, November-December 1983, Vol. XXXII, p. 59.
7. Ulam, Adam, *Stalin* (New York: Viking, 1973) pp. 728 ff.
8. Nieznansky interview.
9. Colton, Timothy J., *The Dilemma of Reform in the Soviet Union* (New York: Council on Foreign Relations, 1984) p. 8.
10. Interview with Zoya Golinskaya.
11. Ibid.
12. Interview with Eugene Koniev.
13. *Pravda*, October 22, 1972; *Pravda*, May 7, 1975.
14. Shevchenko, Arkady N., *Breaking With Moscow* (New York: Knopf, 1985) pp. 184 ff.
15. Golinskaya interview.
16. Dornberg, John, *Brezhnev: The Masks of Power* (New York: Basic Books, 1974) pp. 205 ff.
17. Solovyov, Vladimir and Klepikova, Elena, *Yuri Andropov—A Secret Passage Into the Kremlin* (New York: Macmillan, 1983) p. 168 contains a suggestion that Kulakov committed suicide over failure of his agriculture policy.

18. *Pravda,* July 20, 1982.

3

1. Medvedev, Roy, *Khrushchev* (Garden City, N.Y.: Anchor Press/Doubleday, 1983) pp. 235 ff.; Medvedev, Zhores, *Andropov* (New York-London: Norton, 1983) pp. 48-49.
2. Beichman, Arnold and Bernstam, Mikhail S., *Andropov: New Challenge to the West* (New York: Stein and Day, 1983) pp. 15 ff., 83.
3. *Pravda,* November 28, 1979.
4. *Minutes of Proceedings and Evidence of the Standing Committee on External Affairs and Defense.* Issue No. 95, May 17, 1983. Queen's Printer, Ottawa.
5. Gelman, Harry, *The Brezhnev Politburo and the Decline of Detente* (Ithaca-London: Cornell University Press, 1984) p. 140.
6. *Pravda,* October 22, 1980.
7. *New York Times, The,* May 24, 1982.
8. *Pravda,* February 4, 1981.
9. Beichman and Bernstam, *Andropov: New Challenge to the West,* pp. 98-99.
10. Solovyov, Vladimir and Klepikova, Elena, *Yuri Andropov—A Secret Passage Into the Kremlin* (New York: Macmillan, 1983) pp. 219 ff.
11. *New York Times, The,* January 30, 1982.
12. Medvedev, Zhores, *Andropov,* pp. 8-9.
13. Solovyov and Klepikova, *Yuri Andropov—A Secret Passage Into the Kremlin,* pp. 224-225.
14. Medvedev, Zhores, *Andropov,* pp. 10-11; Gelman, Harry, *The Brezhnev Politburo and the Decline of Detente,* p. 182.
15. Ebon, Martin, *The Andropov File* (New York: McGraw-Hill, 1983), p. 230.

16. Medvedev, Zhores, *Andropov*, p. 15.
17. Solovyov and Klepikova, *Yuri Andropov—A Secret Passage Into the Kremlin*, pp. 191 ff.; Steele, Jonathan and Abraham, Eric, *Andropov in Power* (Garden City, N.Y.: Anchor Press/Doubleday, 1984) pp. 148-149.
18. Beichman and Bernstam, *Andropov: New Challenge to the West*, p. 16.
19. Medvedev, Zhores, *Andropov*, pp. 16-17.
20. Zemtsov, Ilia, *Andropov: Politicheskie Dilemmi i Borba Vlast* (Jerusalem: Vinitsky, 1983) p. 80.
21. *New York Times, The*, November 11, 1982; Solovyov and Klepikova, *Yuri Andropov—A Secret Passage Into the Kremlin*, p. 260.
22. *New York Times, The*, November 16, 1982.

4

1. Zemtsov, Ilia, *Andropov: Politicheskie Dilemmi i Borba Vlast* (Jerusalem: Vinitsky, 1983) pp. 81-82; Medvedev, Zhores, *Andropov* (New York: Norton, 1983) pp. 20-21.
2. Zemtsov, *Andropov*, p. 83.
3. Medvedev, Zhores, *Andropov*, p. 111.
4. Steele, Jonathan and Abraham, Eric, *Andropov in Power* (Garden City, N.Y.: Doubleday, 1984) pp. 152-53.
5. Ebon, Martin, *The Andropov File* (New York: McGraw-Hill, 1983) pp. 240-41.
6. Colton, Timothy J., *The Dilemma of Reform in the Soviet Union* (New York: Council of Foreign Relations, 1984) pp. 34-35.
7. Steele and Abraham, *Andropov in Power*, p. 160.
8. *New York Times, The*, June 16, 1983; Steele and Abraham, *Andropov in Power*, p. 161.

9. Steela and Abraham, *Andropov in Power*, p. 165; *Ekono-micheskaya Gazeta*, No. 41, October 1980, p. 19.
10. Hough, Jerry F., "Andropov's First Year," in *Problems of Communism*, November-December 1983, Vol. XXXII, p. 59.
11. *Minutes of the Proceedings and Evidence of the Standing Committee on External Affairs and National Defense.* Issue No. 95, May 17, 1983. Queen's Printer, Ottawa.
12. Ibid.
13. Interviews with author.
14. Hough, Jerry F., "Andropov's First Year," p. 64; Colton, Timothy J., *The Dilemma of Reform in the Soviet Union*, p. 188.
15. Zemtsov, Ilia, *Andropov: Politicheskie Dilemmi i Borba Vlast*, p. 203; Hough, Jerry F., "Andropov's First Year," p. 57; *New York Times, The*, June 19, 1983.
16. Hough, Jerry F., "Andropov's First Year," p. 59.
17. *Pravda*, April 23, 1983.
18. *Pravda*, July 6, 7, 19, 20, 30, 1983; Hough, Jerry F., "Andropov's First Year," p. 62.
19. *Pravda*, December 17, 1983.
20. Ibid.
21. *New York Times, The*, December 26, 1983.
22. Ibid., February 3, 1984.
23. Hough, Jerry F., "Andropov's First Year," p. 63.
24. *New York Times, The*, February 11, 1984.
25. Ibid.
26. Ibid., February 12, 1984.

5

1. *New York Times, The*, February 17, 1984; Radio Liberty Research 151/84.

2. *New York Times, The,* February 14, 1984.
3. *New York Times, The,* May 1, 1984.
4. *Dagens Nyheter,* May 15, 1984, quoted in Radio Liberty Research 151/84.
5. Radio Liberty Research 151/84.
6. *New York Times, The,* April 12, 1984.
7. Radio Liberty Research 151/84.
8. *New York Times, The,* June 17, 1984.
9. Ibid., September 2, September 10, November 22, 1984.
10. Ibid., October 17, 1984.
11. Ibid., November 22, 1984.
12. Ibid., October 10, 1984.
13. Associated Press, October 24, 1984.
14. Interview with Dwayne Andreas; *The New York Times,* December 5, December 14, 1984.
15. *Sunday Times,* London, December 16, 1984.
16. *New York Times, The,* December 19, 1984.
17. Ibid.
18. *The Guardian,* London, December 18, 1984; *The New York Times,* December 19, 1984.
19. *The Times of London,* December 17, 1984; *The New York Times,* December 17, 1984.
20. *Daily Telegraph,* London, December 22, 1984.
21. *New York Times, The,* December 22, 1984.
22. Ibid., December 25, 1984.
23. Rahr, Alexander, *The Central Committee Secretariat* in Radio Liberty Research 439/84.
24. Associated Press, January 28; February 13, 1985.

6

1. Conquest, Robert, *Russia After Khrushchev.* (New York: Praeger, 1965) p. 6.

2. Gelb, Leslie H., "What We Really Know About Russia," in *The New York Times Magazine*, October 24, 1984.

3. Ford, Robert A., "The Next Soviet Decade," in *Foreign Policy*, Summer 1984, p. 1137.

4. *New York Times, The*, October 24, 1984.

5. Ibid.

6. Colton, Timothy J., *The Dilemma of Reform in the Soviet Union*. (New York: Council on Foreign Relations, 1984) p. 25.

7. Ibid. p. 26.

8. *Minutes of Proceedings and Evidence of the Standing Committee on External Affairs and National Defense*. Issue No. 95, May 17, 1983. Queen's Printer, Ottawa.

9. Ford, Robert A., "The Next Soviet Decade," p. 1134.

10. Colton, Timothy J., *The Dilemma of Reform in the Soviet Union*, pp. 46ff.

11. *The Cambridge Encyclopedia of Russia and the Soviet Union*. Archie Brown, John Fennell, Michael Kaser and H. T. Willetts, general editors. (Cambridge: Cambridge University Press, 1982) p. 54.

12. *Toronto Star*, May 19, 1983.

Index

Solomentsev, Mikhail, 97–98
Solzhenitsyn, Aleksandr, 48
Spain, 93, 111
Spies, 11
Stalin, Joseph, 11, 13, 14, 27,
    28, 29, 30, 32, 35, 46, 47,
    58, 61, 66, 123, 124, 132,
    134, 140, 143, 144, 145
Stalingrad, 28
Stavropol, 15, 23, 28, 29, 32, 33,
    36, 37, 38, 47, 48, 49, 66,
    74, 99, 108
Stavropol Agricultural
    Institute, 33
Suslov, Mikhail, 15, 16, 18, 19,
    23, 27, 28, 34, 41, 42, 48,
    49, 50, 58, 61, 62, 89, 106,
    123, 141, 142

Tadzhik, 144
Taraki, Nur Mohammad, 51
Tashkent, 46, 62
Tatars, 145
Tchaikovsky, 101
Tennessee Valley, 138
Thatcher, Margaret, 13, 16,
    122
Tikhonov, Nikolai, 40, 50, 52,
    58, 59, 68–69, 97, 100, 102,
    105, 108, 116, 128, 136
Togliatti, 140
Toronto, 86
Trotsky, Leon, 13, 21
Trudeau, Pierre, 13, 82, 85, 146
Tsvigun, Gen. Semyon, 63–64

Ukraine, 34–35, 49
United Nations, 53, 145

Ustinov, Marshal Dmitri, 12,
    16, 23, 52, 65, 73, 88, 89,
    95, 101, 102, 108, 111, 115,
    116, death, 122–23; 124,
    125, 126, 142, 146, 148
Uzbek Republic, 62, 144

Vietnam, 15, 145, 146
Virgin Lands, 35, 46, 136
Vishinsky, Andrei, 145
Voroshilov, Marshal K., 28, 62
Vorotnikov, Vitaly, 67, 89, 97,
    99, 143
"Vremya," 79

Warsaw, 55
Warsaw Pact, 112, 128
Westminster, 19, 122
Whalen, Eugene, 85, 87, 136
Windsor, Ont., 86
Winter Palace, 60
World War I, 34, 46
World War II, 27, 58, 124, 145,
    148

Yaroslavl, 75
Yessentuki, 39
Yugoslavia, 92, 141

Zahir, King, 51
Zamyatin, Leonid, 147
Zaporozhe, 35
Zhivkov, Todor, 112, 113, 147
Zhukov, Marshal G., 14
Zia, Mohammed ul-Haq, 82
Zimyanin, Mikhail, 128
Zinoviev, G., 13